TAIWAN

TAIWAN

BY ROBERT GREEN

LUCENT BOOKS
P.O. BOX 289011
SAN DIEGO, CA 92198-9011

Library of Congress Cataloging-in-Publication Data

Green, Robert, 1969–
    Taiwan/ by Robert Green.
        p. cm. — (Modern nations of the world)
    Includes bibliographical references and index.
    ISBN 1-56006-819-1 (lib. : alk. paper)
    1. Taiwan—Juvenile literature. [1. Taiwan.] I. Title. II. Series.
    DS799 .G74 2001
    951.24'9—dc21   00-010390

Copyright © 2001 by Lucent Books, Inc.
P.O. Box 289011, San Diego, CA 92198-9011
Printed in the U.S.A.

CONTENTS

INTRODUCTION
TREASURE ISLAND

Millions of years ago, the shifting earth along the Rim of Fire gave violent birth to the island of Taiwan. From the liquidy, volcanic rock forced above the waves there emerged a landmass that resembled the single wing of a butterfly. Butterflies are, in fact, just one of the natural wonders of Taiwan—the place the Chinese call Bao Dao, or "Treasure Island."

Its semitropical climate makes it a land of mists, through which the dramatic landscape looks like nothing so much as a sublime Chinese painting, half earthly and half dreamworld. The island, located in the East China Sea just ninety miles from the coast of China, was fabled among the Chinese for its natural riches and breathtaking landscape. Through the island runs a north-south mountain range, with rugged peaks falling sharply to deep valleys watered by plunging cataracts. Along the eastern shore, the land flattens and the soil becomes rich and loamy, ideal for cultivating crops.

The island is tiny compared to China, its nearest neighbor. It stretches for just 230 miles from north to south, and it is less than half as wide. It is possible to breakfast on steamed buns and tea in the northern port city of Chi-lung and reach the southernmost tip of the island in time for *wanfan,* the evening rice, as the Taiwanese call dinner.

The island's crops, such as bananas and oolong tea, considered one of the finest of all Chinese teas, have been exported for centuries, but economically Taiwan is foremost a modern nation. It is impossible, for example, to shop in a store in the United States without coming across goods marked with the seal, "Made in Taiwan." Taiwan is a manufacturing powerhouse—the world's leading producer of computer microchips and other high-tech gadgetry—and a rich source of investment capital for mainland China.

Taiwan, the place the Chinese call Treasure Island, is known for its breathtaking landscape.

THE OTHER CHINA

Although Taiwan's population is 98 percent Chinese, Taiwan's relationship with the Chinese mainland is, in fact, the source of Taiwan's greatest anxieties, for China considers Taiwan a renegade province and has threatened to retake it by force.

The conflict stems from the Chinese civil war between Communist and Nationalist forces. The civil war began in 1927 and continued on and off until 1949, when the Nationalists were driven into exile in Taiwan by the Communists, who proclaimed the People's Republic of China on the mainland. On arriving in Taiwan, the Nationalist leader, Chiang Kai-shek, declared that the Republic of China, the Nationalist government, was the sole legitimate ruler of China, but, in fact, it rules only Taiwan.

Today, Taiwan is a land of living history. The Taiwanese military prepares day in and day out for the resumption of the civil war. China has stationed in Fujian province, directly across the Taiwan Strait, a massive assault force and periodically lobs rockets over the island. Taiwan, for its part, has sworn never to rejoin the mainland so long as the Communists are in power, and it drafts its young men for a mandatory military service in preparation for a Chinese assault.

The result is that the Taiwan Strait is one of the most volatile spots on the globe—a possible flash point for a major world conflict. Taiwan, however, is not without its supporters.

Though unrecognized as a country by most of the world, Taiwan is the beneficiary of U.S. military support. And when China makes threatening moves toward Taiwan, the U.S. Seventh Fleet sails into the Taiwan Strait to help ensure that the conflict is resolved peacefully.

THE LITTLE TIGER

The defiance shown by the independent-minded island has shaped much of its recent history. Despite fifty years' warnings from Beijing, the capital of China, Taiwan has developed into a de facto nation. The military rule of the Nationalist Party, complete with its odious martial laws, has given way to a thriving democracy—the first democratic state, in fact, in five thousand years of Chinese history. In the spring of 2000, the Taiwanese elected their first president from an opposition party, peacefully sweeping from power Taiwan's Nationalist Party, which ruled for fifty years. The new president, Chen Shui-bian, declared that Taiwan had stood up, echoing the words uttered by revolutionary leader Mao Tse-tung after he proclaimed the People's Republic of China.

And yet not all Taiwanese are clamoring for complete independence. At the same time that their ambassadors have been dispatched to the countries of the world to gain recognition for the island nation, the Taiwanese have not declared their independence. Many Taiwanese would like to be reunited with the mainland but not until the Communists are ousted.

It may prove that Taiwan has much to teach China. Taiwan already provides China with a model for economic success. As one of the five tiger economies of Asia—countries that have experienced rapid economic development in recent decades—it has already astounded the world by becoming an economic miracle. So too might it eventually provide a model for representative government in China.

THE LAND

To understand why Taiwan has attracted the attention of so many kings and emperors, sailors, adventurers, and refugees, one must understand its geography. Nothing has so determined life in Taiwan as the fact that it is an island. Its climate, migration patterns, even its gods, and most of all its political system, are the result of its being an island.

Taiwan is located in the part of the western Pacific Ocean known as the East China Sea, but the waves of the South China Sea lap the southern portion of the island. Sea boundaries are, of course, not as clearly demarcated as land borders. The island is situated between the latitudes of twenty-one degrees forty-five minutes and twenty-five degrees fifty minutes in the Northern Hemisphere. If Taiwan were located in the Americas, its northern tip would correspond to southern Florida. And the length of the island would stretch through the Florida Keys, reaching at its southernmost point the island of Cuba.

The total length of the island is about 230 miles; its width is just 85 miles at the center of the island, its widest point. Taiwan encompasses 13,892 square miles, which makes it tiny as countries go. Of the world's nations, it ranks number 133 in size. It is about the size of Holland or the combined area of the U.S. states of Massachusetts, Rhode Island, and Connecticut.

Included in the total land area of Taiwan are the island groups of the Pescadores (the P'eng-hu Islands), Jinmen (Quemoy), Matsu, Green Island (Lan Tao), and Orchid Island (Lan Yü), and a host of smaller islands. Jinmen and Matsu lie in the Taiwan Strait close to the Chinese mainland. Kinmen, which means "Golden Gate" in Chinese, is just one and a half miles from the coast of China. Historically, Kinmen and Matsu were considered part of the Fujian province, which lies just across the water on the mainland. These islands are geologically related to the mainland. Lan Tao and Lan Yü, on the other hand, lie off the east coast of Taiwan and were formed the same way as Taiwan itself.

Taiwan's nearest neighbor is China, just 90 miles to the west across the Taiwan Strait. The Philippines are 220 miles south of Taiwan, and the southern Japanese island of Okinawa is 370 miles to the northeast.

Taiwan lays claim to numerous islands in the South and East China Seas. These disputed islands include the Pratas (Tungsha Islands) and the Spratly (Nansha) Islands, which are also claimed by the People's Republic of China, Vietnam, the Philippines, Malaysia, Brunei, and Indonesia. Taiwan also claims the Senkaku (or Tiaoyutai in Chinese) Islands about one hundred miles north of Taiwan. These islands are also claimed by Japan. The value of these disputed islands lies in

Life on Taiwan is greatly influenced by the fact that the country is an island.

P'ENG-HU ISLANDS

Halfway between Taiwan and China in the Taiwan Strait lies Taiwan's largest archipelago, the P'eng-hu Islands. Unlike the lush, mountainous terrain of Taiwan, the sixty-four tiny islands of P'eng-hu are low-lying coral outposts—a barren, windswept terrain marked with occasional tufts of grassland.

The total land area of P'eng-hu is fifty square miles. Though some crops are cultivated—including peanuts, sweet potatoes, and grain—fishing is the mainstay of the islands' economy.

The Portuguese, who landed on the islands in the sixteenth century, called them the Pescadores, or "Fishermen," Islands. But the Portuguese also used the islands as a jumping-off point for expeditions to Taiwan. P'eng-hu, in fact, periodically played host to many hostile forces headed for Taiwan. Dutch, French, and Japanese warships all used P'eng-hu to advance their claims on Taiwan and the water routes surrounding it. Many of the invaders' ships still lie at the bottom of the Taiwan Strait, sunk by the treacherous coral shoals surrounding the P'eng-hu Islands.

their location and their undersea mineral deposits. Taiwanese fishermen frequent the islands, and the discovery of oil deposits under the Senkaku Islands has added new fuel to the territorial claims.

A FIERY BIRTH

As islands go, Taiwan is as beautiful as any other in the Pacific. For a small country, it is a land of wild contrasts. Its breathtaking mountains plummet swiftly to deep gorges, and waterfalls, fed by small, swift rivers, can be seen in many parts of the highlands.

The ruggedness of the landscape is the result of its volcanic birth. Taiwan lies at the intersection of two tectonic plates—the landmass of east Asia and the undersea plate of the western Pacific. When these plates shift, tremors rumble to the surface and sometimes release fiery volcanic lava. Volcanoes are the pressure valves of Earth's molten layers. When pressure builds, a volcano, the visible part of the pressure valve, releases steam, fire, and molten rock, known as lava.

The rugged mountain regions of Taiwan, as seen here in Taroka National Park, suggest the island has volcanic origins.

Geologists still argue over the origins of Taiwan. Is it a renegade bit of landmass that broke off from the Chinese mainland or a volcanic creation sprouting from beneath the sea? The presence of coral from ancient seabeds high up in the mountains of Taiwan suggest that the island had a volcanic beginning, as does the ruggedness of the island's mountains and its hot springs, bubbling up from deep beneath the land.

The question of Taiwan's origin has become political, as nonscientists argue for either the mainland theory or the independent formation theory. These arguments reveal more about whether the postulator believes that Taiwan is politically part of the Chinese motherland or whether it is a separate country. The geological value of such positions is doubtful, and the belief that Taiwan is the result of volcanic activity has gained ground among geologists.

A fact supporting the theory that Taiwan was a volcanic land is its location along the Rim of Fire, a sea region stretching from below the Philippines, through Taiwan, and northward to Japan. This rim of fire is known for its devastating earthquakes, and it corresponds with the fault lines at the edge of the Asian continental plate.

Much like Japan and other islands along the fault line, Taiwan experiences frequent earthquakes. On average, the island is shaken by up to 160 quakes a year. Most of these earthquakes are tremors, which only halt life on the island for a few seconds. Frequently, objects fall from shelves and residents are left fearful of a bigger shock to follow. Occasionally, a large earthquake rocks Taiwan. In 1999, for example, an earthquake measuring 6.7 on the Richter scale shook the island. The quake caused widespread destruction in central Taiwan and caused buildings to collapse in Taipei, the capital.

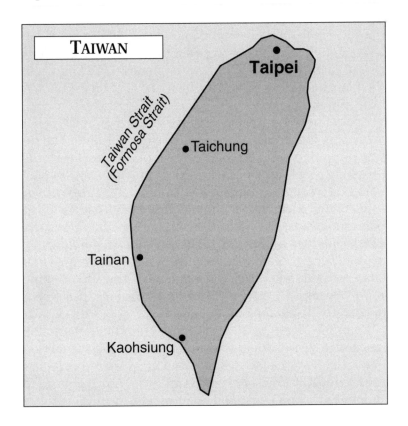

The potential for widespread destruction has caused Taiwan to tighten its building regulations. When the country first modernized in the mid–twentieth century, concrete high-rises were thrown up without regard for the destructive force of Taiwan's lethal and frequent earthquakes. Building codes, however, have been brought up to the standards of Tokyo, also on the Pacific Rim, and Los Angeles, which lies along the San Andreas fault line and experiences frequent earthquakes.

TOPOGRAPHY

The unsettled earth beneath Taiwan is also what gives the island its astonishing landscape. Dramatic mountains sprout up along a north-south axis and run down the island just to the east of center. This is the backbone of Taiwan, and its mountains cover two-thirds of the island. The rock that makes up these mountains is extremely hard. The mountains are covered with dense foliage and receive frequent rainfall. Over the centuries, the many little rivers of the mountains have cut out deep gorges and fantastic formations from the rock. Caves, hissing steam vents, springs, and wild-looking lunar landscapes abound, making the mountains a favorite attraction during the summer months, when the Taiwanese try to escape the heat and gaze on the natural beauty of their island.

The central mountain range drops into a narrow valley before rising again toward the east side of the island. The result is an inhospitable eastern coast of high escarpments dropping precipitously to the sea. There are very few harbors, and an approaching boat would naturally turn north or south to find a way onto the island. This is the least inhabited part of Taiwan, with the exception of two cities along the coast: Hua-lien, in the north, and T'ai-tung, in the south.

The highest peak in the central mountain range is Yü Shan, located smack in the center of the island and reaching 13,114 feet above sea level. There are another fifty peaks near or past the 10,000-foot mark.

From the highest part of the central mountain range, the landscape slopes downward to the west until it reaches a low-lying plain that stretches across the western portion of the island. This is Taiwan's rice bowl—the source of its food supply. This plain is watered by short, swiftly running rivers that originate in the mountains. Very few of these rivers run for any great length, but they are invaluable in watering the rice paddies of the western plain.

The flatness of the western coastal plain gives way to the shallow Taiwan Strait (also called the Formosa Strait), which averages about three hundred feet in depth (as opposed to the plunging depths of the Pacific Ocean off the east coast of Taiwan, which quickly reaches a depth of thirteen thousand feet).

The tidal flats of western Taiwan provide good natural harbors and are still used as major shipping ports, along with the city of Chi-lung, which acts as the port for Taipei in the north of the country.

The majestic Ching-Shui Cliffs of Taroka National Park overlook the Pacific Ocean in one of Taiwan's more spectacular settings.

SUN MOON LAKE

In the central mountain region of Taiwan, twenty-five hundred feet above sea level, Taiwan's most popular lake shimmers like a mountaintop mirage. Its name comes from an apparent compromise of debates on what shape the lake most resembles. From some vantage points, it is said, the lake resembles the round face of the sun, and from others, a crescent moon.

The size of the lake was greatly enlarged when the Japanese occupation forces built a hydroelectric dam nearby. The dam swamped a village of Taiwanese aborigines, but it created what is today Taiwan's most popular honeymoon spot. The clear shimmering waters, mountain mists, and surrounding forests of bamboo, cypress, cedar, and pines give the area a dreamlike atmosphere.

The northernmost and southernmost tips of Taiwan are home to some remarkable natural wonders. North of Taipei lies an area of mixed mountains and coastal beaches. The mountains bubble with hot springs. In the region of Peitao, hot underground springs are channeled directly into public baths and sometimes even directly into hotel rooms. In a place called Hell's Valley, the ground gives way to the bubbling innards of the volcanic rock. Steamy sulfur pits with naturally boiling water attract curious onlookers, who often stop to boil eggs in the natural cauldrons.

Closer to the water, the land gives way to sandy beaches and eerie stretches of yellowish rock, weathered into all sorts of outlandish shapes. The soil is yellowish and looks volcanic. Over the years, wind and water have carved from the stone all manner of strange sculpture. One such structure, for example, is supported by a sloping cone of rock and resembles a head perched atop a sandy neck. This is called Queen's Head, and it resembles the upward swooping headdress of the Egyptian queen Nefertiti.

Similarly, in the south, the lush vegetation and low hills give way to more sandy beaches. This is Taiwan's principal domestic vacation spot. The island ends in a two-pronged peninsula, which is now K'en-ting National Park. The white-sand beaches are the result of eroding coral, and the surrounding rocks have the pockmarked appearance of coral formations, just as spectacular as the northern coast.

CLIMATE

The climate of Taiwan can be thought of as a semitropical version of the British Isles. Like Britain, Taiwan receives frequent rains, but its temperature reaches much greater heights. The result is a hothouse climate.

Taiwan is bisected by the Tropic of Cancer near the midpoint of the island. Most of the country has a semitropical climate, but a slice of the south gives way to the full heat and wetness of the tropics. Altitude is also a factor. A few mountains can sustain snow for brief periods, but the low coastal plains are generally humid and muggy.

The average temperature on the island is about seventy degrees Fahrenheit, but that is deceptive since the temperature usually feels extreme in one direction or the other due to

The tropical climate of Taiwan brings frequent rain showers to downtown Taipei and other parts of the island.

the humidity. The summer lasts from about March or April to September or October and is marked by sweltering heat. The temperature in the north averages about ninety-five degrees, with humidity rarely less than 75 percent. Temperatures are fairly even across the island in the summer, at least in the low-lying areas. Relief from the heat and humidity can be found only in the mountains.

An average annual rainfall of 102 inches makes Taiwan a pretty wet place. Rain is most plentiful in the summer months. There is also more sunshine in the summer, and rain falls in a tropical pattern: Clouds roll in quickly, the skies open, heavy rains fall, and the sun reemerges. It is not uncommon for quick showers to rain down on Taiwan almost daily. Such rapid weather changes are the mark of semitropical and tropical climates.

During the winter months, from about October to February, the temperature varies much more from north to south. In the north, the temperatures average around fifty-six degrees, and in the south about ten degrees warmer. Because of the high humidity, the Taiwanese winter, much like that of Britain, is wet and chilly. The skies are frequently overcast and rain is common.

Both of Taiwan's two seasons receive monsoon winds. During the summer, the winds blow out of the southwest across the South China Sea, and soak the southeastern part of the island. In winter, the pattern is reversed. Winds blow across the Pacific from the northwest, bringing rain to the northern portion of the island.

THE GREAT WINDS

Along with the monsoon winds comes one of Taiwan's most feared and fabled storms: the typhoon. Typhoons have been the curse of sailors in the waters of east Asia since humans first put to sea in that region, and they were responsible for the watery graves of many sailors.

The winds can reach speeds in excess of one hundred miles per hour, whipping up the sea until it is an angry, churning nightmare for a seafarer. Tidal waves grow to such a size that they look like moving walls of water. Ships can vanish from the surface with one crash of these mighty crests.

Taiwan is visited yearly by these wrathful storms. Typhoons often blow down signs, trees, electrical wires, and anything else that is not anchored securely. For coastal towns, and even for Taipei, typhoons can bring devastating floods. In 1968, for instance, a typhoon left Taipei under thirteen feet of water. The word *typhoon* comes from two Chinese characters, *tai* and *feng*, which literally mean "hurricane winds." These words have an almost reverential tone in Chinese, reflecting the fear and respect that the Taiwanese have for these annual visitors.

AGRICULTURE

Taiwan's plentiful rains ensure water for agriculture. Mainland China has always suffered from irregular rains, causing frequent droughts and occasional floods. From ancient times, the Chinese mastered irrigation systems to provide a steady stream of water for their crops. The Taiwanese have transplanted this ancient technology to Taiwan, but it is less necessary because of the regular rainfall.

The combination of fertile, volcanic soil and consistent rainfall has ensured a plentiful food supply for the people of Taiwan. The main crop is rice, the staple of the Chinese diet. This thirsty crop is harvested in the low alluvial plains of western Taiwan, where the combination of rain and irrigation flood the rice paddies. Two to three rice crops can be

Because of plentiful rain and fertile soil, Taiwan produces enough rice to feed its entire population.

harvested a year, and new strains of rice have greatly increased the value of these crops. Taiwan, unlike Japan, produces enough rice domestically to meet the demand of its swollen population. Other crops include a wide variety of vegetables and a famous assortment of tropical fruits, including litchis and mangos. So abundant are the banana crops that the Taiwanese sometimes refer to Taiwan as "the Kingdom of Bananas" (*Xiangjiao Wangguo*). Taiwanese fruits are considered among the finest in the world for their succulent flesh and sweet juices.

THE CREATURES OF TAIWAN

The semitropical climate and rugged landscape of Taiwan have made it home to diverse wildlife. Butterflies are perhaps Taiwan's most famous creatures. They are as numerous as they are varied. These fluttering beauties are sought after in the lowlands and mountains alike by collectors from around the world. Common varieties are seen daily, even in the city.

Taiwan is also the home of a wide variety of birds, from peacocks to sparrows. For centuries the Chinese have had a

LETHAL VIPERS

Local lore has it that the Japanese conducted sinister experiments with venomous snakes during World War II and released these creatures into the wild when they departed in 1945. In any case, poisonous snakes abound in the lush vegetation and semitropical climate of Taiwan. In fact, Taiwan is like a giant living museum of poisonous snakes. Among the venomous snakes of Taiwan are the banded krait, Russell's viper, the Chinese mountain pit viper, coral snakes, and the widespread green bamboo snake. One of the most interestingly named is the "one hundred pacer," which is about how far a bitten person can walk before dropping dead.

The resourceful people of Taiwan have long since put the snakes to good use. Along a two-block stretch, known as Snake Alley, of a Taipei night market, vendors mix a bracing tonic of snake blood and bile extracted on the spot from live snakes. This drink is supposed to stimulate the sexual vitality of men. Likewise, snake soup is also thought to be good for the body.

passion for keeping birds, and old men can still be seen carrying their songbirds in delicate lacquered cages to local parks, where the birds chirp while their owners chatter among themselves.

Larger mammals once wandered throughout the island, far outnumbering humans. But after centuries of being hunted, their numbers have been greatly reduced. The mountains are their last great refuge. Today Formosan black bears, foxes, white-spotted plum deer, and wild boars can still be seen in the forested mountains of central Taiwan.

The most unnerving creatures on the island are surely the reptiles and bugs. At least thirteen species of poisonous snake are found in Taiwan as well as many other less dangerous serpents. There are also lizards of many varieties and, of course, the infernal bugs of the tropics. Taiwan's bugs range from the eerily beautiful praying mantis to a harmless hairy spider that looks like the deadly tarantula. It is a rule that in warmer climates, bugs grow to a larger size. Not only do the cockroaches fly, but if stepped on, the loud crackly crunch is a tip-off to their giant size. There are species that are at least twice the size of the largest cockroaches found in cities in North America and Europe.

Just as the Taiwanese have learned to live with the many creatures of their island, so too have they learned to harness its resources. The island's ruggedness limits the area available for habitation, and the Taiwanese have summoned all of their ingenuity to make life on the island workable for its enormous population of 22.1 million. The high population density of the island has required the diverse peoples of Taiwan to work together; the result is the distinct society of Taiwan.

2

THE PEOPLE OF TREASURE ISLAND

Defining just who the Taiwanese are is a tricky question. Identity in Taiwan is colored by deep political undercurrents, making it difficult even for the Taiwanese to answer the question of who they are. If two Chinese people outside of Asia meet, they will usually ask, "Are you Chinese?" The Taiwanese person will usually answer, "Yes, from Taiwan." If a non-Chinese person asks the same question, the Taiwanese might answer, "No, I am Taiwanese."

At the heart of the matter is the political separation between China and Taiwan. China believes that Taiwan is a renegade province of the mainland, and though it has not controlled the island for more than fifty years, it believes that one day Taiwan will be reunited with China. Accepting that the separation of Taiwan from China is the result of a civil war and that the future of Taiwan is a question for the Chinese and Taiwanese to work out, most nations of the world have concluded that it is an internal problem between two Chinese populations. The result is that Taiwan is not recognized by most nations, and the island, consequently, lingers in diplomatic isolation.

The working diplomatic principle in talks between China and Taiwan, and most outsiders for that matter, is the idea that there is but one China. The "one China policy" has allowed both China and Taiwan to claim for most of their history that each is the rightful ruler of the other. Just as China claims sovereignty over Taiwan, so too did the Nationalist government of Taiwan claim rule over China. The Nationalists, who retreated to Taiwan in 1949, established the Republic of China, which claimed to be the sole legitimate government of all of China.

This is an elaborate fiction agreed to by both Chinese states to save face. No one really thinks that Taiwan is the rightful ruler of China, but the one China policy has allowed the question of reunification between Taiwan and China to be put off until an acceptable resolution can be found.

GOING THEIR OWN WAY

In the fifty years since Taiwan broke away from China, the Taiwanese have developed their own unique identity. Their government and other institutions have been of their own making, and a proud, independent-minded people have created a vibrant democracy of which they are very proud indeed. When the Taiwanese, therefore, say they are Taiwanese and not Chinese, they are expressing pride in the nation they have created. They are stating that they have gone a different way from China and that they are proud of their independence.

The people of Taiwan consider themselves Taiwanese and Chinese.

So what then does one make of the fact that most Taiwanese take great pride in being Chinese? Being Chinese to a Taiwanese is a statement of cultural heritage, and the Taiwanese consider themselves to be the guardians of Chinese culture. Unlike China, Taiwan did not suffer from the excesses of the Communist Cultural Revolution, which sought so vigorously to destroy the ancient social structures of Chinese communities.

In the late 1960s the leader of China, Chairman Mao Tse-tung, unleashed a decade of madness that was supposed to reinvigorate the revolutionary spirit of the Chinese Communist state. During this period, known as the Great Proletarian Cultural Revolution, bands of students, known as Red Guards, rampaged the country denouncing those whom they suspected of abandoning the Communist revolution on

Students and teachers march in support of Chairman Mao Tsetung through Tiananmen Square in Beijing, China, during the Great Proletarian Cultural Revolution in the 1960s.

which the country was founded in 1949. One of the goals of this period was to destroy the remnants of ancient Chinese civilization. Red Guards destroyed Buddhist and Taoist temples and even desecrated the grave of Confucius, China's greatest philosopher.

The Taiwanese, safe on their island fortress, were appalled by the attacks on China's heritage, and contrary to the mainland, considered themselves the guardians of China's rich past. Thus, the Taiwanese, while proud of their independence, also consider themselves to be the direct descendants of thousands of years of Chinese culture.

CONTEMPORARY TAIWANESE

The seemingly contradictory nature of the Taiwanese—culturally Chinese and politically Taiwanese—makes perfect sense to the people of Taiwan. Ethnically, the Taiwanese identify themselves as Han Chinese, a group that encompasses 98 percent of the population of Taiwan. Han Chinese is also the major ethnic group of mainland China. In fact, 98 percent of all mainland Chinese also fall into this grouping.

The Han Chinese are an ancient people who established prehistoric settlements in the fertile river valleys of central

China. Over the centuries, the Han Chinese spread out through most of what is known today as China, but along the way, they intermingled with various other peoples of east Asia. Therefore, the southern Chinese of China's Guangdong province are generally shorter and slightly darker in complexion than the northern Chinese of Beijing and the surrounding areas. This is the result of mingling with various other ethnic groups. In the south these groups included tribes from Southeast Asia, and in the north the Han Chinese mingled with nomadic peoples, such as the Manchus of Manchuria and the Mongols of the Mongolian plateau.

These physical differences are visible in Taiwan, where the Taiwanese population varies in height and complexion, making Taiwan a much smaller version of the diverse mainland. It is important, however, to remember that despite differences in people originating in different areas of China, the Taiwanese consider themselves to be culturally similar and identify themselves as Han Chinese.

But there is a further breakdown of identity in Taiwan. The Chinese population also divides itself into two main groups: the native Taiwanese (*bensheng ren* in Chinese) and the Chinese from other provinces (*waisheng ren*). Although sometimes referred to as different ethnic groups, both are Han Chinese. The difference really lies in the date when they arrived in Taiwan.

THE YAMI OF ORCHID ISLAND

Like other Taiwanese aboriginal peoples, the Yami are descendants of Polynesian seafarers. Their home is Orchid Island, Lan Yü in Chinese, which is located forty miles east of Taiwan's southern tip. The tiny island is a land of rugged beauty ringed by black volcanic shores and battered each year by ferocious typhoons.

To escape the destructive winds, the Yami constructed underground dwellings in the porous rock of Lan Yü. With a population of about 4,250, the Yami are Taiwan's smallest minority group. The remoteness of Lan Yü allowed them to preserve many of their traditions, though Christian missionaries have established churches in almost all major Yami villages. Yami society is matriarchal, and women choose their husbands, who then must continue to prove their worth for fear of divorce.

A NATION OF IMMIGRANTS

Taiwan is above all a nation of immigrants. It is not exactly known when Chinese people first started arriving in Taiwan. As early as the third century A.D., Chinese sailors reached the island, but it was a place still unknown and not at all hospitable. Not until the 1400s, during the Ming dynasty, did the Chinese show an interest in pulling the island into the orbit of the Chinese empire.

By that time, Chinese imperial ships had come into contact with the island, and Chinese fishermen and merchants had already landed on the island. Zhen He, a captain in the imperial navy, is reported to have first introduced the name *Taiwan* to the imperial court. *Taiwan*, which literally means "Terraced Bay," became the name by which the Chinese knew the island. Conquest would come much later, however, and the first Chinese to settle in Taiwan were fishermen who passed through the P'eng-hu Islands in the Taiwan Strait and then sailed on to Taiwan.

THE GUEST PEOPLE

The P'eng-hu Islands, or Pescadores as the Portuguese later called them, became a staging ground for Chinese migration. Two groups of Chinese people migrated to Taiwan through the P'eng-hu Islands. The Hakka were probably the earliest Chinese immigrants, and they still make up one of the main population groups in Taiwan today. *Hakka* literally means "Guest People," a name that reflects their long history of migration.

The Hakka originated in northern, or perhaps central, China but migrated in ancient times to the south. Set off by their own dialect and individual traditions, the Hakka often had a hard time integrating into the local fabric of new Chinese neighborhoods. They were sometimes scorned by other Chinese groups and preferred to stay in closely knit groups, giving jobs to other Hakka. In any case, they developed into a successful merchant and trading class that took to the sea for both trade and fishing.

By A.D. 1000, significant numbers of Hakka Chinese had passed through the P'eng-hu Islands and taken up residency in Taiwan. In later decades, other Hakka would follow. Today, the Hakka make up about 10 to 15 percent of the population of Taiwan. The Hakka, however, have retained their fierce

---

THE GUEST PEOPLE

One group of emigrants from China who have found a home in Taiwan are the Hakka (Kejia in Mandarin). Their name means the "Guest People," and it stems from their long history of migration. The Hakka are often mistakenly called a minority group, but they are in fact Han Chinese, the ethnic grouping of 98 percent of Taiwan's population.

Originating in the Henan province in central China, the Hakka moved southward to avoid famine and other pressures in their native region. They settled in southeastern China, especially the provinces of Fujian and Guangdong (Canton), where they prospered as businessmen and traders. The Hakka also found themselves in the ranks of the secret societies bent on the destruction of the Ch'ing empire. The most famous society member was Sun Yat-sen, who descended partly from the Hakka people.

From southern China, the Hakka sailed for the P'eng-hu Islands and then on to Taiwan as early as 1000 A.D. In Taiwan, the Hakka have prospered, both as farmers and as merchants. Today, they have blended into Taiwanese society. President Lee Tung-hui, the first nonmainlander to become president, is of Hakka origin. And the Hakka dialect is the third most widely spoken Chinese dialect in Taiwan, after Mandarin and Taiwanese.

---

business reputation and are well represented in Taiwan's major industries.

THE *BENSHENG REN*

Close on the heels of the Hakka were sailors from China's Fujian province, which lies directly across the Taiwan Strait from Taiwan. For centuries the Fujianese had made a living from the sea. They too passed through the P'eng-hu Islands and eventually landed in Taiwan. The earliest Fujianese ships created fishing outposts on Taiwan while Fujianese pirates used the island as a jumping-off point to harry ships in the Taiwan Strait and the East and South China Seas. Even after increased immigration from the mainland, the island lay outside the realm of the Chinese emperors, and a hurly-burly society arose around the docks. Pirates hauled in their loot, and local farmers came to sell their extra crops to the sailors.

Emigrants from the Fujian province steadily trickled into Taiwan. Most were escaping economic hardship, and much like European settlers headed for the Americas, they risked the uncertainties of migration in search of a better life. The Fujianese soon outnumbered the Hakka, who were forced to move southward to make room for the new immigrants. Today in Taiwan, the Hakka are still a majority in some towns in southern Taiwan.

These first two groups of Chinese immigrants refer to themselves as *bensheng ren*, or, native Taiwanese. The *bensheng ren* make up about 84 percent of the population of contemporary Taiwan. This number includes about 70 percent Fujianese and a smattering of Chinese from other provinces, and 14 percent Hakka. Although the emigrants from Fujian and the earlier Hakka often clashed, they are both usually considered *bensheng ren* because of their early arrival in Taiwan.

THE *WAISHENG REN*

Native Taiwanese considered General Chiang Kai-shek an outsider.

The most recent wave of immigration to Taiwan was the direct result of the Communist victory on the mainland in 1949, when Mao Tse-tung proclaimed the People's Republic of China (PRC). Defeated in battle, the leader of the Nationalist armies, General Chiang Kai-shek, chose to retreat to Taiwan rather than surrender to the Communists. The remnants of the Nationalist armies as well as many rich landlords, bankers, merchants, and ordinary people fled the new Communist regime. More than 1.5 million Chinese poured across the narrow Taiwan Strait.

The *bensheng ren* call these latecomers the *waisheng ren*, which roughly means "people from other provinces," or simply, "outsiders." The *waisheng ren*, bristling with weapons and lead by a ruthless general, swiftly imposed their will on Taiwan. Chiang Kai-shek proclaimed a new government in Taiwan, the Republic of China, which, he said, was the real government not only of Taiwan but also of China.

Over the last fifty years, most *waisheng ren* have grown to consider themselves Taiwanese. Their numbers are steadily declining. Because of restrictions on immigration from the PRC to Taiwan, there have been few new emigrants from China since the early fifties. The *waisheng ren* now represent about 14 percent of the population of Taiwan. Their numbers are shrinking, but they remain a powerful political force in Taiwan. Most *waisheng ren* reside in Taipei and other major cities and have long enjoyed privileged government jobs.

THE MOUNTAIN PEOPLE

Between the *bensheng ren* and the *waisheng ren*, the Chinese account for 98 percent of the population of Taiwan. But there is also a small minority of non-Chinese people on Taiwan. These are the aborigines, the earliest inhabitants of Taiwan. The *bensheng ren*, or native Taiwanese, are, of course, not really native at all. Neither are the aborigines of Taiwan, but they certainly take the prize for arriving the earliest. And until the seventeenth century, their culture was supreme on the island.

The aborigines are thought to have originated in Southeast Asia. Their features resemble those of the peoples of Indonesia and Malaysia, and their languages resemble Bahasa, the language spoken in Malaysia and Indonesia, which is unrelated to any of the Chinese dialects. The aborigines arrived in the days of prehistory, probably in wooden canoes or ancient sailing vessels. They settled both the low-lying fertile plains of western Taiwan and the rugged lands of the central mountains. They both farmed and hunted for food, wandering and settling as necessary. There are ten aboriginal groups recognized by the Taiwanese government today. They make up about 2 percent of the population of Taiwan, and three tribes alone, the Ami, the Atayal, and the Paiwan, make up 85 percent of the aboriginal population.

As Chinese emigrants landed on Taiwan and appropriated the lowlands for farming, the aborigines were forced to retreat into the mountains. The remaining tribes became isolated in tiny mountain villages. This phenomenon is revealed in the Chinese word for the aborigines. They call them the *shandi ren*, or "mountain people."

The earliest inhabitants of Taiwan, the shandi ren, *pictured here in traditional tribal clothing, make up about 2 percent of the population today.*

The Taiwanese government has instituted a number of legal protections for the aborigines in an attempt to preserve their cultures, but their numbers are shrinking. Today some have assimilated into Taiwanese society, speaking Chinese and seeking jobs outside their own communities. But many retain their tribal heritage, and the government is considering creating autonomous regions for them to continue in their own fashion.

SPOKEN CHINESE

The aboriginal peoples of Taiwan continue to speak their native dialects, but through contact with the Chinese, they have also begun to speak Taiwanese. Taiwanese is the most widely spoken dialect in Taiwan. Outsiders often mistake it for a distinct language; however, it is neither a separate language nor the official language of Taiwan.

Taiwanese is a dialect of Chinese, the mother language of all Chinese people. But Chinese is a language of a handful of major dialects and hundreds of smaller local dialects. The differences between Chinese dialects are significant. A speaker of one dialect will not understand a speaker of another dialect. The Taiwanese dialect hails from the southern Fujian province. In Chinese, it is either called *Taiwan hua* ("Taiwanese") or *Minan hua*, the dialect of the area south of the Min River in Fujian.

Taiwanese is a direct offshoot of the southern Fujian dialect (*Minan hua*), but through centuries of separation, Taiwanese has adopted new words and idioms. Taiwanese is in the process, in terms of linguistic evolution, of becoming its own dialect of Chinese.

The official language of Taiwan is Mandarin Chinese. Mandarin is one of the most widely spoken dialects in China. It is spoken by the people of Beijing and the surrounding

REN QING WEI

The Taiwanese have a habit of greeting each other with the question: "*Ni chi guo le ma?*" ("Have you eaten yet?") This is an example of what the Taiwanese call *ren qing wei*, which can be translated as "the flavor of human feeling." *Ren qing wei* is a paramount consideration for the interaction among Taiwanese, and when one Taiwanese asks another if he or she has eaten, it is an attempt to extend hospitality and foster an atmosphere of *ren qing wei*. The question, however, is not just a formality—a meal, or at least a snack, will often follow.

Ren qing wei is the recognition of the need for etiquette and traditions of an ancient people. And the demonstration of *ren qing wei* says something profound about a person. Most of all, it gives face, or respect, to both parties. The Taiwanese will often attempt to reject the effusive offers of a meal or sweets so as not to put their host out. But allowing the host to prevail in the end is considered an example of good *ren qing wei*. The concept is often confusing to outsiders, but it is an essential component of the Chinese social system. *Ren qing wei* must, above all, be accompanied by sincerity, as empty formalities will cause both parties to lose face.

northern provinces. Mandarin is also the official language of the People's Republic of China.

When the *waisheng ren* arrived in Taiwan in 1949, they spoke a collection of dialects since their ranks were drawn from all corners of China. But even though southerners out-numbered northerners, the Nationalist Party made Mandarin Chinese the official language of China. This was a political statement. If the Nationalist government were to return to the mainland one day, it should preserve all of the functions of the official government, including the national language. In Taiwan, Mandarin Chinese is called *guoyu*, which literally means the "national language."

Mandarin Chinese today is the dialect of schools throughout Taiwan and of government-sponsored news stations. It is the most widely spoken dialect in Taipei, where many *waisheng ren* still live. Taiwanese, however, is becoming more accepted, even for official purposes. More and more children of the *waisheng ren* also speak Taiwanese, and more native Taiwanese now serve in the government. In fact, Taiwan's last two presidents were both born in Taiwan and alternated between the Taiwanese and Mandarin dialects in their public speeches.

WRITTEN CHINESE

The differences between Mandarin and Taiwanese (as well as all other Chinese dialects) are fortunately limited to the spoken language. One of the great unifying forces of Chinese civilization, both in Taiwan and in China, is that the Chinese written language is the same for all dialects. That means that a Mandarin Chinese speaker and a Taiwanese speaker who could not understand each other's spoken tongue could simply write a note. The written Chinese would be immediately understood by both.

It is one of the greatest wonders of the Chinese language that the speakers of two different dialects could read aloud the same page of a book, and to a listener, they would be speaking entirely different dialects. But both readers would be reading and understanding exactly the same thing. It is also important to note that neither is translating into their own dialect. In other words, they are both reading the writing that they use every day. It just happens to be the same for both of them.

Mandarin Chinese will most likely remain the official language of Taiwan, but Taiwanese speakers have come to expect that the children of *waisheng ren* will speak Taiwanese as well. For example, if a young *waisheng ren* jumps into a taxi and gives directions in Mandarin, the cabbie will sometimes give his fare a quick rebuke for not speaking Taiwanese. After fifty years of Nationalist Party rule, and to some extent *waisheng ren* domination, the native Taiwanese are shouting out loud for more respect and, for the most part, they are getting it.

The differences between the native Taiwanese and the *waisheng ren* represent the long history of immigration to Taiwan. Taiwan has provided a jumping-off point for fishing vessels for thousands of years, and its strategic position just off the coast of China has also drawn the attention not only of the Chinese but also foreign powers.

3

A Prize for Kings and Emperors

Until the sixteenth century, Taiwan avoided the direct control of any single power. China, more concerned with matters at home, declared a ban on migration to Taiwan and only occasionally put an imperial ship to anchor in Taiwan's ports. But emigrants from Fujian continued to make the crossing, and the Chinese population grew.

Life on Taiwan continued unhampered by outsiders. The Chinese ran small businesses, serviced the ports, and harvested rice. They employed members of their own families and clans, and life continued in a semifeudal state. The aborigines, still uncowed by the Chinese incursions, continued to roam most of the island, still outnumbering the Chinese.

Taiwan caught the attention of the outside world only when a ship foundered on her shores and the crew went missing. It was discovered that the tattooed and leathery-skinned aborigines liked to make a prize of the heads of shipwrecked sailors. Fear of the mountain people spread, along with exaggerated tales of the barbarous yowls and savage cruelty of the headhunters of Taiwan.

To add to Taiwan's lawless reputation, pirates looted passing ships with far more regularity than the headhunters won their trophies. The Chinese pirates raided the sea lanes between China, Japan, and Southeast Asia, which ran near their island hideaways. However, these were really part-time pirates, who alternated between piracy and legitimate maritime trade. As one writer puts it, "When times were good, they traded. When times were bad, they raided."[1]

Fire-Breathing Galleons

In 1517 the captain of a Portuguese galleon sighted a new island en route to Japan and recorded in his ship's log a land he called Ilha Formosa, or "Beautiful Island." That island was Taiwan, and by the end of the century the Portuguese, hungry to strengthen their position in the waters of Asia, had established a trading colony on the northern part of the island.

Europe in the sixteenth century was undergoing a re-markable period of expansion. It was a time of intellectual curiosity and voracious appetites for wealth. And the mon-archs of Europe dispatched their deep-hulled sailing ships to seek out the riches of the world. The ships carried adventur-ers in search of gold, royal cartographers, scientists, and mis-sionaries, who attempted to spread the Christian faith around the globe. When the European ships dropped anchor in far-flung ports, they negotiated for lucrative trading rights. When these were denied, they often opened up with their shipboard cannons or dispatched a squad of armed sailors to take what they were not given.

The Portuguese had already established a trading port in the Chinese city of Macao, over which they raised their own flag. Taiwan proved to be a passing fancy, and they soon abandoned Ilha Formosa.

THE RED-HAIRED BARBARIANS

No sooner had the Portuguese left than the Dutch, the next of Taiwan's European suitors, arrived. The Dutch already had vast holdings in the island groups of Southeast Asia, an em-pire that included parts of Malaysia and Indonesia. The Dutch, under the banner of the Dutch East India Company, shipped the wealth of these countries back to Europe. The Dutch East India Company was a commercial firm, awarded exclusive rights to the Far East trade by the Dutch monarchy.

By way of the P'eng-hu Islands, the Dutch arrived in Tai-wan. Unlike the Portuguese, they decided to stay. For their capital, they chose the tiny port city of Anping (modern-day T'ai-nan City) and constructed in 1624 a massive fort with red-tiled roofs and whitewashed walls punctuated with can-nons. Fort Zeelandia became the administrative center of the colony of Taiwan, conceded to the Dutch by the Chinese court.

Dutch rule of Taiwan produced some good results. The Dutch built roads, modernized the harbors, dug wells, and created some law and order. But the Chinese chafed at being ruled by these red-haired barbarians, as they called them. To the Chinese, the Dutchmen looked like demons. The black-haired Chinese found the reddish hue of some of the Dutchmen's hair to be otherworldly. They recoiled at their height and the sight of limbs, chests, and faces sprouting with hair.

The Chinese have, since ancient times, believed that China was the center of the civilized world. The traditional name for China, the Middle Kingdom, reflects this cultural arrogance. The Chinese considered all people not enlightened with Chinese culture to be barbarians and expected them to bow to Chinese superiority. The Chinese on Taiwan shared this exalted opinion of themselves and preferred self-rule or rule by China to the government of the strange Dutchmen.

Dutch policy also provoked the local population. From Java, in the Dutch East Indies, the Dutch imported opium to Taiwan. The black substance was extracted from the flower pods of poppies. When smoked, it produced a powerful narcotic effect, leaving the smoker in a trancelike state. As the practice of opium smoking spread on Taiwan, the Chinese elders worried about the destructive effects on the Chinese community.

The Chinese resented even more the imposition of heavy taxes by their Dutch masters. True to the colonial system, the Dutch billed the Chinese for having a Dutch government. Moreover, farmers had to rent land and farming implements from the Dutch. Faced with the unjust Dutch government, the Chinese community on Taiwan revealed a trait for which they are still known today: rebelliousness. They organized armed insurrections, which were put down by the Dutch, sometimes with the help of the aborigines.

The Dutch also faced threats from other European powers. In 1626 Spanish galleons landed on the northernmost tip of Taiwan and established a foothold on the island. They built a fort in Tan-shui and used the harbors near Chi-lung. The Spanish, like the Portuguese and the Dutch, had already established trading links with Japan and China. Alarmed at the growing presence of the Spanish on Taiwan, the Dutch responded in 1642 by bombarding Spanish positions and drove them off the island.

THE CHANGING OF THE MANDATE OF HEAVEN

Shortly after the Dutch booted the Spanish out of Taiwan, China itself faced invasion from a foreign enemy, an invasion that would have a profound effect on the development of Taiwan.

The ruling dynasty of the mainland, the Ming, had proven to be one of China's greatest dynasties. The Ming court encouraged the spread of Chinese arts and culture, and pride in being Chinese rose to new heights. The Ming dynasty had grown weak and corrupt, however. Court intrigues plagued the capital at Beijing, and imperial rule throughout the country weakened.

Just as the Ming court was teetering, a new enemy appeared on the northern border. In 1644 Manchu horsemen pierced the Great Wall, the defensive barrier that stretched for two thousand miles across China's northern frontier.

Stretching two thousand miles across northern China, the Great Wall was not enough to keep out the Manchus in 1644.

The warlike horsemen swept down on Beijing under their war banners. The Manchus, also called the bannermen, sacked Beijing, and the last of the Ming emperors hanged himself.

The Manchus happily subscribed to the Mandate of Heaven, the Chinese concept of divine rule, and established the Ch'ing dynasty (1644–1911). The Chinese were appalled. Were not they the sons of heaven and, as the Middle Kingdom, the most advanced people on Earth? The humiliation of conquest was almost unbearable. Many Chinese loyal to the Ming dynasty fled southward and some reached Taiwan. The Ming court appealed to a wealthy Taiwanese pirate by the name of Cheng Chih-lung to command the remnants of the Ming forces. Cheng operated at will in the Taiwan Strait because the Manchus were unfamiliar with naval warfare. Cheng ferried many escaping Ming loyalists to Taiwan and conducted raids along the coast.

THE ISLAND FIEF OF THE PIRATE KOXINGA

The elder Cheng eventually defected to the Manchus, but not before his son Cheng Ch'eng-kung could take up the work. The young Cheng was the son of a Japanese mother, whom his father had married during one of his trading voyages to Japan.

Cheng was truly a product of the cosmopolitan nature of the Pacific trade routes. According to historian Jonathan D. Spence,

> His father's trade networks extended from Nagasaki to Macao, and in their fortified home near Amoy (Xiamen) could be found a chapel with both Christian and Buddhist images, as well as a bodyguard of black slaves, fugitives from the Portuguese at Macao. Access to the inner living quarters of the compound was made directly by boat.[2]

To fund his war against the Manchus, Cheng traded in silks, sugar, spices, and other goods. He was as good at making money as he was at sacking ships. Cheng proved to be a brilliant naval commander, and the Ming royal family rewarded him with the use of their own surname. He is known to history therefore as Koxinga, a rough romanization of the Taiwanese pronunciation of the imperial name.

Koxinga is considered a hero for driving the Dutch out of Taiwan in 1662.

In 1659 Koxinga attempted to retake the great southern capital of Nanjing from the Manchus. The Manchus proved to be unbeatable on land, and they sent the naval wizard back to the sea. This put an end to any serious attempts to retake China in the name of the Ming dynasty.

Sailing back to Taiwan, Koxinga turned his wrath on the Dutch. With a force of thirty thousand armed men and spies who knew the Dutch fortifications, Koxinga razed the Dutch

SECRET SOCIETIES

Secret societies have played an important role in Chinese history for hundreds of years. Originally, they were formed to plot the overthrow of the emperor. Their members, having no open voice in the political life of China, found solidarity in their secret brotherhood. The leaders of the Nationalist revolution, including Sun Yat-sen and Chiang Kai-shek, found support in these societies and joined their ranks.

After the 1911 revolution, some of these societies turned to lucrative criminal enterprises and became a feared force in Chinese life. Nowhere did the secret society play such a role in the criminal undercurrents of twentieth-century China as in Shanghai. The Green Gang, originally an anti-Manchu society, took the helm of Shanghai's trade in opium, prostitution, gambling, extortion, and kidnapping. So influential was the leader of the Green Gang, a ruffian named Big-Eared Tu, that even the foreign community of Shanghai treated him like the local governor, and the French, in fact, made him a member of the municipal council.

Chiang Kai-shek got his start as a member of the Green Gang, which later smashed Shanghai's Communist movement through violence and murder, all at the behest of General Chiang.

---

settlements, killing Dutchmen and enslaving their women. He then laid siege to Fort Zeelandia, the center of Dutch power. In 1662, the Dutch, massively outnumbered, surrendered, leaving to Koxinga the trade goods and treasures of Fort Zeelandia, worth 1 million ounces of silver.

Four decades after the Dutch arrived, Taiwan was free of all foreign influence. Koxinga had restored Taiwan to the people of the Middle Kingdom. He died the same year, half-mad and much celebrated. He is still considered a hero in Taiwan.

INTO THE FOLD

Koxinga's son and then grandson ruled Taiwan in a short-lived dynasty. They cultivated respect for the Chinese classic writings on government and philosophy and encouraged calligraphy and other Chinese arts. Some historians have argued that the Chengs established the first truly Chinese government on Taiwan.

But the dream was not to last, for the family had made too many enemies on the mainland. After quelling southern China, the Manchus turned their attentions on Taiwan. One of Koxinga's former lieutenants, Shi Lang, was recruited to command a Ch'ing naval force, thus using the bandit naval tactics on the bandits. In the steamy month of July 1683 Shi Lang launched a war fleet of three hundred vessels. This force, sailing under the Ch'ing imperial standard, first sacked the P'eng-hu Islands and destroyed the backbone of the Cheng navy. On arriving in Taiwan, the Chinese residents decided that resistance was pointless and surrendered.

The Emperor Hsüan-yeh, one of the mightiest Ch'ing emperors, decreed that Taiwan was to be a prefecture of Fujian province and deposited a garrison of eight thousand soldiers in Taiwan to enforce imperial decrees. After two centuries of self-rule and occupation by foreign powers, Taiwan found itself a part of the great Chinese empire. Rule from the mainland by the Manchu Ch'ing dynasty was preferable to rule by the foreign devils. However, the Chinese of Taiwan continued to harbor dreams of restoring the Ming dynasty to China, and frequent rebellions broke out.

Chinese administrators seemed to consider Taiwan a bad posting, and they often frittered away their time on the island smoking opium or pursuing other entertainment. The Taiwanese were often left to their own devices in solving trade disputes and other matters. The Ch'ing court seemed content with the arrangement and took little interest in the island. It even banned emigration from the mainland to keep Taiwan a backwater.

During the Chinese rule of Taiwan (1684–1895), however, the population increased dramatically. Residents of Fujian blatantly ignored the imperial decree, and many set sail for Taiwan. In 1831 a Prussian missionary recorded: "The island has flourished greatly since it has been in the possession of the Chinese."[3] By 1886, the population had surpassed 2.5 million. The Chinese population had finally outstripped the number of aborigines, and the Ch'ing court elevated Taiwan to provincial status. Taiwan, from that point on, would be known in China as the twenty-second province of China, a claim the government of China still asserts today.

THE CHINA TRADE

In the late–eighteenth century, Western ships began buzzing around the Chinese coast. The emperor treated them with high-handed contempt, making the delegations of Europe and the United States bow in a ritual known as the kowtow. The emperor simply refused to see the benefit of trade with the foreign barbarians, who had ghostly pallors and demonic light-colored eyes and were clad in stiff-collared clothing.

When the emperor attempted to put an end to the foreign ships, the British responded by shelling Chinese cities and destroying the Chinese imperial navy. The victory in the two Opium Wars in the mid–nineteenth century opened the way for unrestricted trade with China for all Western nations.

Although the Chinese were not much interested in foreign products, they consumed large quantities of opium, which the British had been flooding into the country to redress the trade imbalance. That imbalance was caused by the voracious appetite for Chinese things in Europe and America. Chinese tea took its place in the daily life of the British and is now associated as much with England as with China. Fashionable society also clamored for porcelain dishes, known as china, and for fine silks from which to make dresses, curtains, and other luxuries.

The growing trade in tea created a demand for faster ships since tea leaves lose their flavor over time. American shipbuilders in New England responded with the clipper ship, the fastest trading vessel of its day. Clippers, such as the *Nightingale, Witch of the Waves*, and the *Cutty Sark*, set speed records along the trade routes to China and greatly enriched American merchants, who were an increasingly large part of the China trade.

THE OPIUM WARS

Chinese control over Taiwan, however, was to come to a startling conclusion at the end of the nineteenth century. The Ch'ing dynasty had grown weak and corrupt like the Ming before it, and Western ships pressed claims on the China trade with renewed hostility.

At the root of the China trade was opium, the same curse that the Dutch had brought to Taiwan. When Europeans began trading with China, they discovered that the Chinese had little use for the trade goods of the barbarians. The British paid in silver for the many Chinese goods—such as tea, silk, and porcelain, which had become such a rage in fashionable Europe—while making no money in return.

To redress the trade imbalance, the British struck on the devilish idea of exporting opium from their Indian colony and selling it to the Chinese. Opium smoking on the mainland took root, and demand skyrocketed as the addictive drug did its handiwork on the Chinese. Soon the British were making a fortune at the expense of the well-being of the Chinese.

To stamp out the growing opium trade, the Chinese emperor dispatched a righteous and incorruptible Mandarin scholar-official named Lin Zexu. Commissioner Lin confiscated and set fire to the British opium stores in the southern port city of Canton.

The outraged British responded by shelling Canton into submission. The British argued that the principles of free trade enabled them to sell whatever goods they wished to the Chinese and that these principles were worth defending.

Two wars, known as the Opium Wars, were fought over the opium trade. In both conflicts, the British easily destroyed Chinese opposition and went about their business trading

The British declared war on China when the Chinese emperor attempted to block imports of opium.

Weak and defeated from the war with the British, China was no match for the invading Japanese.

opium. In the Treaty of Nanjing, which ended the first Opium War, the British declared that more Chinese ports should be opened to Western ships. These "treaty ports," as they were known, included four Taiwanese shipping centers: Chi-lung, Su-ao, T'ai-nan, and Kao-hsiung.

The British also imposed crushing financial penalties for the costs of the war and the loss of profits in the opium trade. The Americans, not wanting to miss out on a good thing, sued the Chinese government to make the ports open to all foreign traders. This broadminded American approach ensured that all European nations, as well as the United States, would also profit from the opium trade.

The humiliating defeat at the hands of foreigners was to have drastic consequences for China's last dynasty. The Ch'ing had been proven weak and corrupt. Clearly they had lost the Mandate of Heaven, and anti-Manchu feeling swelled in China.

It was in this atmosphere of uncertainty and discontent that the Japanese arrived on the scene. Japan, unlike China, had embraced the technology that had arrived in Asia and made the Westerners with their gunboats so invincible.

Japan had modernized quickly and was feeling particularly warlike by the end of the nineteenth century.

Wanting to carve out their own piece of China, the Japanese attacked in 1895. They struck at Korea, a possession of China. The Sino-Japanese War allowed the Japanese to show off their newly modernized army and navy. They delivered a crushing defeat in Korea, sinking the Chinese navy. A country that the Chinese had always considered backward and insignificant had just laid low the great Chinese empire in one fell swoop.

The Chinese sued for peace and signed the Treaty of Shimonoseki, a humiliating document written by the Japanese.

THE SOONG FAMILY

There is perhaps no family that had a greater influence in shaping China's republican revolution than the Soong family. The patriarch of the family, Charlie Soong, arrived in the United States as a child and ran away from his uncle's tea and silk shop. Penniless and in a strange land, Soong found support from the Methodist Church and a stern hero of the U.S. Civil War named General Julian Carr. Carr had Soong educated at Trinity College (later Duke University), and Soong adopted the Christian faith of his benefactors.

Returning to China, Soong made a fortune publishing bibles for China's growing Christian population. With this fortune, he bankrolled the Nationalist revolution of Sun Yat-sen against the Ch'ing government.

His six children were to carry on the revolutionary work, propping up revolutionary leaders with money and companionship. Soong's three sons became financiers of the revolution. As the richest banking family in China, they both paid for the revolution and drew financial and military support from abroad. T. V. Soong, the most prominent of the brothers, served both as prime minister and foreign minister in the Nationalist government. The three Soong sisters were not to be outdone by their brothers. Soong Ai Ling became the guiding light of the family and a power broker in her own right. Soong Ching-ling married Sun Yat-sen, twenty-six years her senior. She later served in the Communist government. Her sister Soong May-ling married Chiang Kai-shek and became the goodwill ambassador to the United States, where she won the affections of President Franklin D. Roosevelt. In 1949, she became the First Lady of Taiwan.

The Japanese were rewarded for their military adventure with Korea, Taiwan, and the Ryukyu Islands, which lie between Japan and Taiwan. After more than two hundred years of Chinese rule, Taiwan once again found itself the prize of a foreign power.

UNDER THE RISING SUN

Upon hearing the news that they were now citizens of Japan, the Taiwanese decided that they were having none of it. They took up arms and prepared to give the Japanese a hot reception. Over seven thousand Chinese soldiers died resisting the Japanese occupation forces, and the point was driven home that just as China was no match for the Japanese war machine, neither was Taiwan.

The Japanese established a colonial government and martial law. Resistance, which continued throughout the entire length of the occupation, was dealt with severely. Resistance members were shot or beheaded with samurai swords. In 1915, for instance, during the Tapani Revolt, the Japanese murdered ten thousand Taiwanese.

Although the Japanese did not colonize Taiwan in the sense of encouraging emigration from Japan to the new possession, they did try to remake Taiwanese society in the likeness of Japan. Japanese civil administrators rewrote the curriculum of Chinese schools. Japanese was taught instead of Chinese. And Chinese schoolmasters were forced to sing the praises of Japan's history. Taiwan became a harsh and orderly place for the first time in its history. The calm that existed on the surface was enforced with the threat of violence.

In some respects, the Japanese influence benefited Taiwan. The Japanese modernized industry, built hospitals, laid railroad tracks, and improved harbors. Japan also constructed hydroelectric generators, making the Taiwanese the first Asians outside of Japan to have electric power. Electric power meant factories, and electric factories meant a boost in industry.

Even in agriculture, the Japanese increased production. They introduced strains of rice from Japan and expanded the rice-growing areas. The Japanese genius for efficiency also led to expanded harvesting of timber and bamboo. Unfortunately for the Taiwanese, the Japanese exported most of the fruits of this industrial boom back to Japan, where it was fueling the imperial Japanese army.

Taiwan benefited from Japanese occupation in some ways, including the construction of new buildings in Taipei.

THE RAYS OF THE RISING SUN

Japan's victory over China in 1895 marked the beginning of one of the most ruthless military adventures the world has ever seen. Braced by their success and believing in their own superiority, the Japanese began to dream of an empire that would stretch across east Asia. By 1932 the Japanese had moved from Korea into the northern part of China known as Manchuria. Manchuria was rich in iron ore and other resources, and Japan needed them for its expansion. Weak and divided, the Chinese accepted the Japanese occupation of Manchuria. But Japan's success only sharpened its appetite. In 1937 Japan created an excuse to invade China, and soon Japanese troops were rushing headlong down the east coast of China—murdering, raping, and looting in a mad frenzy of war lust.

Taiwan fed the Japanese military with its natural resources. "Now Taiwan was supplying Japan with great amounts of industrial products, from wood pulp and chemicals to copper and foodstuffs," writes historian Spence. "Its already impressive network of airfields was being expanded, as were docking facilities at Keelung [Chi-lung] and Kaohsiung [Kaohsiung], and the entire railroad network."[4] It was bad enough that the Japanese were forcing the Taiwanese to equip the Japanese in their war on China, but worse was to come.

On December 7, 1941, the Japanese bombed the American naval base at Pearl Harbor, Hawaii. The United States immediately declared war on Japan, turning Japan's conquest of Asia into a world war. The Japanese flag, a red sun on a white background, was changed to the red sun with rays emanating in all directions. This was the Japanese war flag, and it indicated that the Japanese were striking out like the rays of the sun.

Taiwan's natural resources supplied Japanese military campaigns against China and the United States.

The Japanese seized Singapore, Hong Kong, Burma, French Indochina, and the Philippines. Their advance stopped only on the edge of British India in the west. To fight on such an enormous front, the Japanese needed more and more

soldiers. They turned to Taiwan. Taiwanese men were drafted into the Japanese military and forced to fight other Chinese. Many resisted and were hanged.

Toward the end of 1944 the Allied forces were successfully driving the Japanese off the islands of the Pacific. As they neared the Japanese home islands themselves, they bombed Japanese bases on Taiwan. In the end, the Japanese were stopped only by the horrors of a new weapon, the power of which the world had never witnessed. On August 6, 1945, the U.S. bomber *Enola Gay* dropped an atom bomb on the Japanese city of Hiroshima. The city vanished in a single flash of light and fire. Another bomb fell on the Japanese naval base at Nagasaki three days later. Japan surrendered unconditionally. After fifty years of Japanese occupation, Taiwan was once again its own master.

4

A REPUBLIC IN EXILE

On October 25, 1945, Taiwan officially returned to Chinese control. That day, celebrated in Taiwan as Retrocession Day, did not, however, return Taiwan to imperial control. While Taiwan had languished under Japanese occupation—the political aspirations of the Taiwanese put on hold—China had undergone the greatest political upheaval in its history. A revolution in 1911 had overthrown the weakened Ch'ing dynasty and established the first Chinese republic. The republic was established along the principles of the revolution's founder, Sun Yat-sen.

Sun was a man who dreamed only of peace. He was almost certainly the most humble and unselfish leader ever to rise to power in China. Soon after becoming the president of the Republic of China, however, Sun was shoved out by a warlord named Yüan Shih-k'ai, who hoped to promote himself to the exalted position of emperor.

The situation in China deteriorated. Warlords—generals with private armies—controlled much of the northern part of the country. The Nationalist government, led by the ruling Kuomintang, or Nationalist Party, loosely controlled much of the south from its capital at Nanjing. The situation was further complicated after 1927 when the Chinese Communist Party began to attract adherents among the workers of China's cities and the peasants of the sprawling countryside.

The incompatibility of the Communists and Nationalists led to the Chinese civil war. Although partly interrupted by World War II, the civil war flared up again immediately after 1945. This civil war led to the last great wave of immigration to Taiwan, and it would also reshape the nature of the Taiwanese state.

FRIEND OR FOE?

To bring Taiwan under Nationalist rule in 1945, the leader of the Kuomintang, General Chiang Kai-shek, dispatched a governor-general to the island. The man Chiang chose to institute Nationalist rule on Taiwan was Chen Yi, a warlord who had joined the Nationalist armies early in the civil war. Chiang could not have chosen more unwisely. Chen was a ruthless man who considered the Taiwanese collaborators for supplying the Japanese during the war. To Chen, it made no difference that the Taiwanese had no choice in the matter, or that anti-Japanese resistance movements more generally reflected the sentiments of the people of Taiwan. "In the mood of victory over Japan," writes one historian, "[Taiwan] was considered both a fat piece of 'war booty' and a 'remote province.'"[5]

It was this view of Taiwan as war booty that most upset the Taiwanese. Chen settled old debts and made a handsome profit dismantling and selling off Taiwan's industries. Much of the industrial development in Taiwan was the product of

Sun Yat-sen, founder of the greatest revolution in Chinese history, dreamed only of peace.

Japanese occupation, but instead of restarting it for the benefit of the island, Chen looted the country and sold the goods back in China.

The Taiwanese were outraged, fearing that the new governor was little better than the Japanese. Nor was Chen's attitude singular. Many of the Nationalist civil and military administrators treated the Taiwanese with contempt. After fifty years of being forced to learn Japanese, Taiwanese citizens who were heard speaking the language were treated harshly. Governor Chen, who himself spoke Taiwanese and Japanese, refused to communicate in any tongue aside from Mandarin Chinese, which not many Taiwanese spoke at that time.

Taiwanese resentment of the Nationalist attitudes finally boiled over on February 28, 1947. Two plainclothes Nationalist policemen were patrolling

*Some Taiwanese found
life with Nationalist
governor Chen Yi
(saluting, second from
right) worse than life
under Japanese rule.*

the streets of Taipei when they came across a Taiwanese
woman selling cigarettes without a license. Cigarette sales
were restricted by a government monopoly, making the
woman, in the eyes of the police, a black marketeer. In an act
of senseless cruelty, the two policemen beat the woman to
death. An outraged crowd quickly gathered, and the policemen fired into the crowd, killing four persons.

This incident, known as 2/28 Day, ignited widespread ri-
oting among the Taiwanese. Their bottled frustrations finally
uncorked, they terrorized anyone who spoke Mandarin and
beat to death a number of people. Governor Chen responded
with a swift and savage counterstrike reminiscent of the
Japanese occupation. On March 8, Nationalist troops massacred thousands of Taiwanese, perhaps as many as twenty
thousand, thereby putting an end to the protests.

RETREAT

Chen Yi's legacy on Taiwan was to instill resentment among the native Taiwanese for the Nationalist mainlanders, a sentiment that has not entirely dissipated even today. This was unfortunate considering the events that were unfolding in China.

Despite substantial aid in money and arms from the United States, the Nationalist armies under Chiang Kai-shek suffered defeat after defeat by the mainland Communists. The Communists fielded highly motivated soldiers and attracted large swaths of China's population to their cause.

Few of China's peasant farmers probably understood the principles of Communism at the time, but they did understand how they were treated by the Communists. Mao ordered the communist soldiers—known to the Communists as the People's Liberation Army and to the Nationalists as Red Bandits—to treat the common people with the greatest of courtesy. When passing through a village, they were instructed to pay for room and board and for whatever they ate. This was in sharp contrast to the Nationalist soldiers, who dealt with peasants high-handedly and often forced villagers to join their army at gunpoint.

The Communists, in other words, won the propaganda war. Never before in Chinese history had any ruling power

2/28 PEACE PARK

The February 28, 1947, incident, when Nationalist troops massacred Taiwanese citizens, was not always a recognized holiday in Taiwan. In fact, for decades the government stifled all discussion of the incident and forbade historians and newspaper reporters from writing about it.

Only with the end of martial law under Chiang Ching-kuo in the 1980s did the history of the brutal incident once again play an open part in Taiwanese politics. The growing freedom for scholars resulted in open debate about the incident. The government, bowing to the pressures of Taiwanese society, initiated its own investigation and published a report condemning the atrocity in 1992. President Lee Tung-hui commissioned a statue commemorating 2/28 Day in Taipei's New Park, which was later renamed 2/28 Peace Park by Taipei's mayor, Chen Shui-bian, who later became president of Taiwan.

stopped to ask the peasant what he wanted. Never before was the peasant treated as an equal. The result was a huge groundswell of support for the Communists.

Chiang, on the other hand, was crippled by his own militaristic personality. He believed that orders should be followed unquestioningly. He also represented the landlord class of China, which feared that the Communists would seize its land and its hereditary privileges. For the same reasons, Chiang also attracted the support of rich bankers, industrialists, and anyone else with financial interests to guard from the Communists. This fact ensured that the Nationalists had plenty of money, but it caused resentment among the masses of China.

By early 1949 the Nationalists were losing badly on the mainland, fighting rearguard actions and retreating toward the coastline in the south. By the end of the year, the Nationalists had retreated across the Taiwan Strait to Taiwan. More than 1.5 million Nationalist mainlanders flooded into Taiwan. These are the *waisheng ren*, who took control of the island's politics for the next half-century.

NATIONALIST TAIWAN

The native Taiwanese were none too happy with the wave of refugees that landed on their island, especially because the Nationalists took the best jobs in Taiwan, not only in government but also in the private sector. They imposed their will on the people of Taiwan as ruthlessly as the Japanese had and were greatly resented by the native Taiwanese.

Fearing that the Taiwanese could rise in revolt, Chiang Kai-shek took a number of steps to improve relations with the Taiwanese. The first was to deal with the legacy of the 2/28 Day incident and the hatred for the governorship of Chen Yi. Chiang had Chen paraded out to the Taipei racetrack in June 1950 and executed him by firing squad.

Chiang also instituted land reform. He redistributed Taiwan's farmland to give more people a chance at ownership. Unlike the Communists, Chiang paid the former owners of the land, avoiding the bitterness that the Communist land reform policies left in China. Chiang's policy led to the creation of a class of people with extra money floating around. This money was invested in industries and small businesses. The policy jump-started Taiwan's economy, priming it for future

success. Chiang's fostering of the Taiwanese economy would be his greatest legacy, for he encouraged the Taiwanese through liberal business laws and heavy government subsidization. Politics was another matter altogether.

Chiang Kai-shek tried to appease the Taiwanese by instituting land reforms, such as redistributing farmland.

The government of the Republic of China (the Nationalists) was founded on three principles Sun Yat-sen had laid out earlier in the century: *mintsu* (nationalism), *minchuan* (democracy), and *minsheng* (economic progress and security). These principles were written into the constitution of the Republic of China and were generally supported by the Nationalist government in Taiwan.

Although Chiang was staunchly anti-Communist, democracy was alien to him, and he soon showed himself to be an authoritarian leader. In Taiwan, Chiang suspended the constitution. He outlawed criticism of the Nationalist Party, censored the news, and ruled Taiwan like a police state. He argued that martial law was necessary because the Republic of China was still at war with the Communist mainland.

Chiang believed that the Nationalist government's home on Taiwan was a temporary affair, and he constantly referred to the right of the Nationalists to govern all of China. But the mainland also hoped to put an end to the civil war, and it wanted to do it by force.

RELATIONS WITH THE UNITED STATES

American leaders publicly supported Chiang, praising him as a defender of democracy. In private, however, there was much criticism for the state of martial law in Taiwan. Foreign policy advisers questioned the wisdom of supporting a dictatorship in the name of democracy.

The reason for this public-private divide lies in the changing state of world affairs. After World War II, the United States

THE XI'AN INCIDENT

Between the 1911 revolution and the end of the Chinese civil war in 1949, warlords became a meddlesome, sometimes fearsome, challenge for all Chinese leaders. They were men of varied character. One warlord named Fung Yuxian became known as "the Christian General" for his ardent faith and his humanitarian treatment of his soldiers. Another, Zhang Zuolin, who was known as "the Manchurian Bandit," became the most powerful man in north China during the 1920s.

In 1936 one of the northern warlords, Zhang Xueliang, was so infuriated that the Chinese were fighting among themselves while the Japanese ravaged the country that he took matters into his own hands. Zhang was allied with Chiang Kai-shek and was acting in coordination with Nationalist troops to suppress the Communist Red Army. After being ordered to attack the Communists in the north, Zhang instead lured Chiang to the ancient capital at Xi'an. In Xi'an, the warlord launched a surprise attack on Chiang, who was eventually captured in a cave clad only in a nightshirt and shivering from the cold.

Zhang then forced Chiang to agree to a truce with the Communists and a renewed effort to drive the Japanese from China. The architect of the Xi'an Incident, as the event is known to history, ended up a prisoner of Chiang Kai-shek after the war. He lived the rest of his life under house arrest in Taiwan and attended the same Christian church as his former captive.

and the Soviet Union both attempted to promote their philosophies of government. The result was the Cold War, in which the champions of democracy and Communism prepared for war through an arms race, building nuclear weapons and dispatching forces throughout the world. As a Communist state, China was clearly in the Soviet camp, although the two countries were never the best of friends. The Americans, therefore, used Taiwan as a counterweight, a Chinese government opposed to Communism and friendly to the West. And the little island figured largely in U.S. foreign policy.

In 1950 the Cold War flashed into a hot war on the Korean peninsula. Communist North Korea invaded democratic South Korea. The United States, under the banner of the United Nations, went to war on the side of the South while China backed the North. China saw this as an opportunity to invade Taiwan. Mao ordered China's armed forces into Fujian province, just across the Taiwan Strait, where they assembled an invasion force of small boats. To prevent their ally from falling to the Communists, the Americans ordered the U.S. Seventh Fleet into the Taiwan Strait.

The move was risky, for it was tempting China into a direct war with the United States. But Mao decided that his fledgling navy was no match for the American destroyers and abandoned the invasion. The United States had taken Taiwan under its defensive umbrella, ensuring the survival of Chiang and the Nationalists.

In the coming decades, the United States would back up its protection of Taiwan with defense treaties. In 1955 the U.S. Congress passed the Sino-American Mutual Defense Treaty, and in 1979, just after the United States formally recognized the People's Republic of China and severed diplomatic ties with Taiwan, Congress passed the Taiwan Relations Act, which continued American military support for the island although it was no longer recognized politically.

CHIANG CHING-KUO

Under Chiang Kai-shek, the people of Taiwan experienced a rise in the standard of living, the foundation of a forward-looking economy, and the negotiation of security arrangements with the United States. But for a greater political role, the Taiwanese had to wait for the general's death.

Chiang died in April 1975, still clinging to the hope of the Nationalist government returning one day to reclaim all of China. For more than twenty-five years he had nursed the dream, all the while restricting Taiwan to the rule of one party: the Nationalist Party, also known as the Kuomintang (KMT).

Chiang's power passed to his eldest son, Chiang Ching-kuo. The transfer of power followed the letter of the constitution, but many Taiwanese resented that power had passed from father to son. It resembled nothing so much as a modern dynasty. There was no reason to suspect that Chiang Ching-kuo would deviate from his father's authoritarian policies. He had never expressed pro-democracy tendencies when he served in the government under his father. Moreover, he had spent part of his political education in the Soviet Union, where surely the Soviets pointed out the failings of the Western democracies.

Chiang Kai-shek's son, Chiang Ching-kuo (pictured), assumed power upon his father's death.

THE LEGACY OF THE BLUE SHIRTS

In the 1930s Chiang Kai-shek became enamored with the military aura of the German and Italian Fascist parties. Nationalist officers were dispatched to Germany and Austria to study Fascist methods. When they returned, they displayed a zeal for the goose-stepping tactics of the Fascists. Order has always been highly prized in Chinese society, and Chiang Kai-shek always favored strict military control, despite the praise he received from Western powers as a champion of democracy.

His admiration for the Fascist techniques of Germany and Italy prompted Chiang to establish his own corps of loyal political enforcers and intelligence agents. This group was called the Blue Shirts, a reference to the Nazi Blackshirts of Germany. The Blue Shirts, operating under the deceptive title of the Investigation and Statistical Bureau, assassinated opponents of the Nationalist government and extracted information through torture.

In 1947 Chiang brought the successor of the Blue Shirts to Taiwan. The new agency blended law enforcement with counterespionage. Its headquarters in the Hsintien suburb of Taipei became a feared place, where opponents of the government were interrogated with cruel techniques. As Taiwan's government opened up in the 1970s and 1980s, the more sinister aspects of the bureau were eliminated, and today Taiwan has a security service resembling the American Federal Bureau of Investigation or Britain's Scotland Yard.

To everyone's surprise, Chiang quickly set out on a policy to reshape Taiwan's political system. In response to native Taiwanese demands for more representation—the *bensheng ren* still resented exclusive rule by the *waisheng ren*—Chiang encouraged more native Taiwanese to join the Nationalist government. His father had started the trend, facing the same pressures, but now Chiang Ching-kuo seemed to be leveling the playing field. More and more native Taiwanese were elected to the legislature.

At the same time that President Chiang was opening the system to democratic reforms, an opposition party was gaining steam. Taiwan's first opposition party was the Democratic Progressive Party (DPP). The DPP drew supporters from mainly native Taiwanese citizens who hoped to reclaim a voice in ruling their own land. DPP candidates also gained support for their anticorruption drives and advocacy of independence for Taiwan. This last point—the question of declaring full independence for Taiwan—was certainly the most controversial. China has always said that if Taiwan declares independence, it will invade the island.

In the election of 1986, DPP candidates became the first opposition politicians elected to (and allowed to sit in) the legislative branch of Taiwan's government. Chiang, to the surprise of all, had opened Taiwan's political system and even encouraged the opposition, all at the cost of his own party's monopoly on power. This was a radical shift in Taiwan's political history. As historian John F. Copper puts it, "It reflected Taiwan's rapid evolution away from an authoritarian, one-party political system toward competitive democracy."[6]

The new political freedoms were the result of a set of major reforms undertaken earlier that year by Chiang at the Nationalist Party's Central Committee conference. At the meeting, Chiang not only called for the legalization of opposition parties but also for the easing of press restrictions and other "suspensions" in the constitution. In short, Chiang had just lifted the state of martial law that had been in effect since 1949.

LEE TUNG-HUI

Through his willingness to open up the ruling Nationalist Party, Chiang Ching-kuo is held in high regard by most Taiwanese even today. His father, whose statues and pictures are featured throughout Taiwan, was considered a man of fierce convictions and admired for protecting Taiwan from the Communists. His son, however, was remembered most of all for giving the Taiwanese some say in their own government.

To put an end to Chiang family rule, Chiang Ching-kuo declared that none of his family members should take office after him. This was a well-received gesture, and when Chiang died in 1988, he was succeeded by Vice President Lee Tung-hui. Lee's rise to the presidency was a turning point in itself. Not only did it end rule by the Chiang family, but Lee was a native Taiwanese. The Nationalist Party had so successfully recruited native Taiwanese citizens that they now represented its leadership. The Nationalist Party, at least for a time, had ensured its own survival in an open political process by including native Taiwanese politicians.

Lee continued the democratization that had begun under Chiang Ching-kuo. Taiwan began to take on the trappings of a Western democracy, with protests, showy electioneering stunts, and special-interest groups that represented the interest of, for example, farmers or laborers.

In 1994 a change in the constitution called for the direct election of the president. Previously, Taiwan's president was elected in parliamentary fashion. In other words, the ruling party, the Nationalists, had always chosen the president in their own closed votes. Lee, however, was directly reelected by the people of Taiwan to be their president in 1996. This was the first time that the people of Taiwan had ever chosen their own leader and, in the words of one historian, "the first popular election of a chief executive in 5,000 years of Chinese history."[7]

Taiwan had evolved since 1949 from a one-party state controlled by a general to a successful democracy with a strong economy and a vibrant culture of its own.

5

TAIWAN TODAY

A stranger visiting one of the major urban areas of Taiwan will most likely be struck by the din of Taiwan's city life: the cries of street hawkers, the sounds of building construction, the beeping of horns, and the high-pitched scream of the ubiquitous motor scooter. Most of all, a stranger, even from one of the world's major cities, will probably be struck by the throngs of people.

With a population density of about 1,580 persons per square mile, Taiwan is one of the most densely populated countries on Earth. The unique culture of the Taiwanese is partly the result of living in close quarters for thousands of centuries, both on the mainland and in Taiwan. From early times, mainland China has been densely populated. Although China is a vast country, most of it is not hospitable to settlers. The result was that China's east coast sustained the bulk of its population. Chinese people therefore had to learn to live together in close-knit communities. This is one of the most noticeable characteristics of Chinese and Taiwanese life.

The love of company expresses itself in many ways that markedly differ from Western countries. Dining is a visible example. The Chinese prefer to eat at a large round table. This ensures that everyone has an easy time chatting with the other diners. Food is served from large dishes placed in the center of the table. Meals are rarely served á la carte. The Taiwanese in fact think there is something barbarous about closely guarding a single plate of food as Westerners do. Instead, they share. Each dish is sampled from the platters in the center of the table, and it is good manners to serve others at the table from the platters.

And rarely do the Chinese eat in silence. There is an expression for the ideal atmosphere of a Chinese restaurant. It is *re nao*, or "hot din." A meal is often a festive occasion, with loud conversation and sizzling, steaming dishes served from the kitchen throughout the meal. A typical restaurant meal reflects the atmosphere of life in Taiwan, for the hot din can be found in the night markets, on ordinary streets, and in Taiwan's many karaoke establishments.

The chaotic feeling of *re nao* seems to fit in nicely with the remarkably modern living conditions in Taiwan. Most families have cars or motor scooters and live in modern apartments, and Taiwanese teenagers are rarely seen without their cell phones and frequently communicate by e-mail. In certain

Taiwan is one of the most densely populated countries on Earth.

The Chinese prefer to dine at round tables and to share their food using platters placed in the center of the table.

ways, the high standard of living, in fact, makes Taiwan resemble Japan more than China.

But beneath the hot din of modern life in Taiwan, beneath the surface of modern conveniences and high-tech gadgets, lie some ancient cultural traditions. This contradiction is one of the most striking facets of life in Taiwan. Not only are the Taiwanese culturally conservative, but they live day in and day out with some of the most ancient aspects of Chinese culture.

To understand the nature of Taiwanese society it is important to look at the great philosophies and religions that have shaped its cultural identity. The three greatest strains of thought that still shape the lives of the Taiwanese are Confucianism, Buddhism, and Taoism. The Taiwanese do not make clear distinctions between philosophy and religion. Nor do they necessarily have to choose between different creeds. In fact, most Taiwanese observe both Buddhist and Taoist rites, and no one would discount the pillars of Confucianism, which hold up the most basic aspects of Taiwanese philosophy and social customs.

THE FLAVORS OF CHINA

When the various peoples of China arrived in Taiwan, they brought with them their local cuisines. This makes Taiwan a convenient place to sample the flavors of China, and the Taiwanese love nothing so much as eating.

Regional cooking imported from China falls into three main categories. Northern cuisine differs from other regions by its reliance on grains. Wheat flour is used to make noodles, buns, breads, and fried pancakes. The dishes are generally heavier to compensate for the colder climate. Some specialties are stuffed buns, dumplings, thick bean soups, and, of course, Peking duck, the most celebrated dish of all of China. The next major regional cuisine comes from the fertile valleys of Sichuan and Hunan in central China. The dishes are famous for their various peppers, making it the hottest of all Chinese food. The last great regional cuisine is more recognizable to Westerners. Cantonese food, from southern China, is slightly more mild than other regions and is known for its many kinds of sauces. Like the dishes of Sichuan and Hunan, the dishes are based on rice or rice noodles.

The Taiwanese have also developed a number of local specialties, including stewed pigs' feet, three-cup chicken, and many dishes with bean curd, or tofu. Among the most-loved meals is the Mongolian barbecue, a meal that includes many meats and vegetables cooked in front of the diners and is famous for its rich flavors and all-you-can-eat portions.

Products seen in Taiwan's food markets reflect the diversity of their cuisine.

THE THOUGHTS OF MASTER K'UNG

Confucius, China's most famous philosopher, was a member of the scholar-official class of government administrators. To gain a government post in ancient China, a scholar had to pass a series of exams, which included Chinese poetry, history, and the writing of essays using a writing brush in a particular calligraphic style. This examination system for government jobs created an interesting alliance between scholars, teachers, and the government. The ideal government official was both a scholar and a ruler.

Confucius became a prime example of the scholar official. He was born in 551 B.C. to the K'ung family and rose quickly through the state examination system, eventually earning the distinction of being called Master K'ung (Kongzi in Chinese, which was romanized to Confucius). Confucius was most concerned with the relationship of the officials to the people and the people to each other. His philosophy is really a model of social organization. Every person in the empire had a role in Confucius's philosophy. A man had to be at once a good husband and father and a loyal subject of the emperor.

The basic unit of the system was the family. From the family, the responsibility of every Chinese citizen then expanded outward to the village, the province, and finally to the emperor, who was seen as the father of the nation. Confucius believed that society would function smoothly if each person acted properly in his or her role. This was quite a conservative idea, for it encouraged each person to be content with his or her station in life.

Confucius laid out the basic principles that governed the relationship of different stations in life: The student must respect the teacher, the son and wife must obey the father, the subject must obey the emperor. This philosophy pleased the emperor and all those in power in China. It is essentially a model for the preservation of the existing order of things. The peasant is content to be a peasant; the wife is content to listen to her husband.

Confucius is most widely known for his many sayings, through which he revealed his theories of a harmonious society. These sayings were published in the *Analects of Confucius.* For example, Confucius wrote that children who treated their parents with respect were unlikely to revolt against the emperor and, in Confucius's view, the established order of the universe.

CONFUCIUS AND THE FAMILY

Although Confucius's teachings did not always match the reality of human experience, his influence can be seen even in contemporary Taiwan. Most Taiwanese, for instance, still respect their parents, and family devotion is a mark of a good son or daughter. This manifests itself in many ways in modern Taiwan. Parents still have a say in what course their children's lives take: which schools they attend, what careers they follow, and whom they marry.

In the past two decades, social restrictions in Taiwan have loosened a bit, and young people have made great strides toward, for example, choosing their own spouse. Other aspects of family devotion retain their original importance, as is the case with caring for the elderly.

As parents grow old, they are not packed off to a nursing home, or any other home for that matter. Most Taiwanese

While social customs have loosened over the last twenty years, responsibility and devotion to family has remained of utmost importance to the Taiwanese.

A TAIWANESE WEDDING

Weddings are important ceremonies in Taiwanese society. The traditions of Confucius weigh heavily on the proceedings, which are elaborate and must be followed to ensure the success of the match.

According to the teachings of Confucius, offspring are required to carry on a family's traditions. If there are no children, no one will care for the graves of the ancestors and their spirits will roam the earth hungry and angry.

The legal aspect of a wedding is the least important part; it is generally limited to a little paperwork at city hall. But the wedding banquet is of greatest importance, and families will nearly bankrupt themselves to throw a banquet of grand proportions. Nearly everyone whom the family has ever known is invited to the banquet, not only extended relatives but also business associates, old schoolmates, and illustrious members of society. The person with the highest social standing—if you are lucky, perhaps the mayor of the town—will preside over the short ceremony that indicates that the union is official. Speeches and toasts are then made throughout a ten-course meal by anyone else who wants to speak.

During the banquet, the bride changes her attire up to a dozen times, reappearing with each new look to the applause of the diners. Red is the favored color; white is used only for funerals. To show their appreciation for the guests' attendance, the bride and groom share a toast with every table in the banquet hall, an exhausting and intoxicating ritual.

families still live with several generations under one roof. Generally, the eldest son will remain in his parents' home (which he will eventually inherit). His wife will join him, and they will raise their children with the help of his parents. Daughters, on the other hand, generally move in with the parents of their husband.

The benefit of this system is that the elderly are cared for by their own families; they neither need money from the government nor do they risk the chance of becoming homeless. It is considered a great shame—to oneself and one's family—not to care for the elderly members of the family.

Just as Confucius had advocated, the family remains the primary unit of social organization in Taiwan. If a member of a family needs money to buy a house, he will turn first to his family. Even overseas relatives will send large checks to finance the education of a distant member of the family. The well-being of each family member reflects on the prestige of the entire family.

BUDDHISM

If most Taiwanese can be described as Confucian in outlook, they can be described as Buddhist in religion. Buddhism arrived in China in the first century A.D. by way of India. After reaching China, Buddhism was promoted or discouraged by various emperors, but among the common people its influence continued to grow. The Chinese molded Buddhism to their own liking, and it quickly took on a distinctly Chinese quality. The first sect of Buddhism to take root in China was Zen Buddhism, known as Chan Buddhism in China.

Located on Light of Buddha Mountain, this enormous gold Buddha statue symbolizes Buddhism, the religion practiced by most Taiwanese.

Although all Buddhist sects believe that spiritual matters take precedence over life on Earth, Chinese Buddhism is markedly more earthly than in other places. The Taiwanese are a practical people, and their faith reflects their tendency to hedge bets. A Taiwanese Buddhist will pray at a temple for assistance in all sorts of earthly pursuits. A templegoer might burn incense and perform *bai bai*—prayers performed by clasping the hands together and bowing several times—to appeal for good luck in business, marriage, or to pray for a place at a good university for a son or daughter.

This is not to say the Taiwanese are not true believers, but they have adapted Buddhism to suit Chinese sensibilities. Nevertheless, some Taiwanese, especially elderly Chinese, devote much of their time to Buddhism's teachings, attending weekend retreats, and visiting temples daily.

More commonly, however, the Taiwanese visit Buddhist temples when they are in need of guidance. Festivals, births, deaths, and other important occasions in Taiwan also require a visit to the temple. This is a matter not just of religion but of propriety. It is simply the expected thing to do, and following social expectations is taken very seriously in Taiwan. It helps continue thousands of years of history, and it brings honor to the family.

TAOISM

Intermingled with Buddhism in Taiwan is Taoism. Literally, Taoism is the belief in the way, or the Tao, which leads one toward a harmonious existence with nature. Taoism is older than both Confucianism and Buddhism and was begun by a librarian at the imperial archives who is known as Lao-tzu, which means "Old Master." Lao-tzu taught that people should find harmony with the changing rhythms of nature. It is both a philosophy and a religion, and it has greatly shaped the mind-set of the Taiwanese.

In the West, Taoism is most recognizable by the yin-yang symbol, which combines a black and a white swirl flowing into each other, with an eye of white in the black and an eye of black in the white. The symbol represents the two sides to nature: night and day, death and life, cold and hot, feminine and masculine. These sides, according to Taoism, are natural parts of human nature and the wider world. One cannot ex-

THE GODDESS MATSU

Among the many gods of Taiwan, Matsu is, perhaps, the most important. She is the protector of fishermen and seafarers, and for an island nation, this makes her an important part of Taiwanese life. Her importance is shown by the 385 temples dedicated to her. The oldest of the temples is located in Makung, in the P'eng-hu Islands, the traditional stopping-over point for ships headed to Taiwan.

It is believed that Matsu was a real person, who lived, perhaps, during the ninth century. She was the daughter of a fisherman in the Chinese coastal province of Fujian. According to legend, she left her body one night while sleeping and rescued her two brothers from a typhoon.

The image of Matsu can be seen throughout Taiwan, usually seated with a crown and holding a scepter. She is called on not just to protect seafarers but also to aid in the delivery of children and for many other common concerns. Her birthday on the lunar calendar is a major holiday in Taiwan.

---

ist without the other, just as day cannot exist without night, and each flows into its opposite.

The Tao is visible in the even-tempered approach the Taiwanese have adopted in everyday life. Although the Taiwanese are generally conservative, they are also accepting of people who are not like them. The temperance of their outlook is often attributed to Taoism, which teaches that all things are in transition and that one should not cling too rigidly to a set of ideas. Taoism can also be seen in the traditional methods of exercise practiced by many Taiwanese.

SPORTS AND EXERCISE

The Taiwanese have inherited some of the word's most fascinating methods of exercise from mainland China. These exercises are directly based on Taoist teachings of the yin and yang and resemble meditation more than the carefree sports of the West.

The most popular form of exercise in Taiwan is tai chi chuan, which translates to "grand ultimate boxing." Tai chi resembles slow-motion fighting in which the practitioner executes a series of memorized movements while breathing slowly and deeply. Although the movements are based on fighting techniques, including punches, kicks, and blocks, tai chi is practiced for health and tranquillity.

Taiwan's many public parks are the favorite place to practice tai chi, and the preferred time is the early morning, when, according to Taoism, the trees and plants give off vital energy, which can be inhaled by the tai chi students. The sight of early morning tai chi practitioners can present a spectral, otherworldly impression, as the human shapes run through their silent movements in the light of the rising sun.

Tai chi is particularly popular with the elderly since it stretches the muscles and improves circulation. The more vigorous forms of martial arts are popular among young people. Kung fu still holds an honored place in Taiwanese society. Kung fu incorporates the beliefs of Taoism, but it is also connected to Buddhism. The most famous school of kung fu, Shaolin kung fu, originated in a Shaolin Buddhist monastery in central China. Impoverished children were generally left at the door of the temple to be raised and trained by the monks. To their religious training was added an acrobatic form of fighting known today as Shaolin kung fu. Shaolin and many other styles of fighting are still widely practiced in Taiwan, and teachers are revered by their students, almost as much as fathers.

The Taiwanese have also adopted a number of Western sports. At school, children play soccer, basketball, baseball, badminton, and tennis. But it should be noted that school is for studying in Taiwan, and sports take a distant second place. Because of the low value placed on the professional athlete, most children are discouraged from placing too much stock in sports. A few sports, however, have gained favor among Taiwan's wealthier families. Golf is played on the expensive real estate of Taiwan's country clubs, and skiing on the few snow-clad slopes of the highlands has also gained enthusiasts in recent years.

EDUCATION

The low value placed on sports is a direct reflection of the high value placed on education in Taiwan. With a literacy rate of over 90 percent, the population of Taiwan is highly educated and highly skilled. Compulsory education lasts for nine years, but most students continue on. So important is

*Wang Shi-Ting (right)
and Lee Janet-Whids of
Taiwan celebrate their
gold medal in women's
team tennis at the
thirteenth Asian Games
in Bangkok, Thailand,
in 1998.*

education in Taiwan that one of the five branches of Taiwan's government is devoted solely to promoting learning in the country.

The Taiwanese have inherited the Chinese reverence for education, and teachers are as highly valued as moneymaking businessmen. It is a matter of family pride for children to do well in school, and parents often put great pressure on their children starting at an early age. Everything about the early years of school in Taiwan encourages serious study. Classes are held generally from 8 A.M. to 5 P.M., with a half day on Saturdays.

Students are expected to participate in their own education. This occurs by taking an active role in the classroom and the corporate life of the school. When students arrive at school in the morning, they are addressed by the principal and then they sing the national anthem. The corporate atmosphere continues when students break up into their particular groups of classmates. Students generally spend months, and sometimes years, with the same classmates. It is not unusual, therefore, that Taiwanese adults still have friends from grade school.

School in Taiwan is paid for directly by families through tuition. This keeps taxes low and inspires a direct involvement of parents in their children's education. Parents will often tutor their children, as will extended members of the family. The general spirit of education in Taiwan is communal. Subjects also reflect the unifying nature of Taiwanese education. Students rigorously memorize famous Chinese poems and study classics of Chinese literature. This ensures a certain continuity between the generations, a certain core subject matter, which must be mastered in order to be considered an educated person.

Education is greatly revered in Taiwan and children are expected to assume serious study at a young age.

Along with liberal arts classes, students are expected to study sciences: chemistry, biology, physics, and computers. Students who do well in these subjects move on, through a competitive examination system, to technical schools or to

one of Taiwan's universities. Taiwan has excelled in producing mathematicians and scientists who have fueled the high-tech economy.

ARTS AND CULTURE

Part of every Taiwanese student's curriculum is the art of calligraphy, the writing of the Chinese language with ink and brush. The goal of mastering the traditional form of Chinese writing is more than just good penmanship. It is considered one of the highest arts of Taiwan. The art is largely imitative, and calligraphers have been practicing the five basic styles—seal script, clerical script, standard script, semicursive script, and cursive script (also known as the running style)—since ancient times.

The surviving works of the old masters of Chinese calligraphy are used as ideal models and give the calligrapher something by which to judge his or her work. Calligraphy was considered one of the marks of an educated man, and even today politicians display their own calligraphy as a demonstration of their virtue and education.

The tools of calligraphy were famous in their own right. Known as the four treasures of the study, calligraphy tools include the writing brush, the bristles of which are made from the hair of boars and other animals; the ink stick; the ink stone, on which the ink is mixed; and paper, a Chinese invention. These treasures are often very beautiful, and even the paper, made from rice pulp, is of a fine texture so as to show every stroke of the brush.

The same tools are used for Chinese painting, and the painter is expected to be a master calligrapher as well. Chinese painting celebrates the beauty of nature, and its representation strives to show the state of harmony that exists between the painter and his subject. Painting is an art heavily influenced by Taoism, and the painter allows an invisible force to guide his brush. As one master explains, "He who deliberates and moves the brush intent upon making a picture misses to a still greater extent the art of painting, while he who cogitates and moves the brush without such intentions, reaches the art of painting."[8] Chinese art is known for the subtlety of its colors and the dreamlike representations of natural landscapes. People generally figure only as a tiny part of a landscape, reflecting the humble position that people hold to nature, according to Chinese philosophy.

Traditional Chinese painting is widely practiced in Taiwan today. It has also been transformed to incorporate techniques of modern art. The disregard for representational painting has made this transition somewhat natural, and today Taiwanese painters also paint in stark modernist styles. With the opening up of Taiwan's political system in the past three decades, art has also become a means for expressing political sentiments.

Taiwan represents a vivid example of a culture that has preserved its traditions while smoothly adapting to the modern world. It is considered one of the most socially conservative places in Asia, but it is also one of the region's most technologically advanced economies. And Confucianism coexists with a hurly-burly democratic system.

AN UNFINISHED STORY

6

It is one of the great ironies of Taiwan's modern history that the more successful it becomes, both economically and politically, the more it provokes Chinese threats of war. China is determined to regain control of Taiwan, which it still considers to be a renegade province.

Feeling in Taiwan is mixed on the subject. Many *waisheng ren*, who arrived after the Chinese civil war ended in 1949, have retained a longing to see some kind of reunion with China, especially since some of them still have relatives on the mainland. Most native Taiwanese, however, desire either complete independence or a loose connection with China that permits Taiwan to steer its own destiny.

FORTRESS TAIWAN

At present, Taiwan retains sovereignty over its own affairs, but it suffers from life in the shadow of China. Despite a thriving democracy and a roaring economy, Taiwan is ostracized by the world community. Most nations, including the United States, have refused to recognize Taiwan as an independent nation in deference to China. China is not only a regional military power but also an important trading partner of many of the world's nations. Most nations have preferred to keep their relations with China on a good footing by not recognizing Taiwan.

Most countries have accepted the Chinese position that Taiwan's relationship with the Chinese motherland must be worked out between the two Chinese states. But the support for the Chinese position is not absolute. The United States has told the Chinese that the dispute must be resolved peacefully, and it has backed up its words with the

U.S. Seventh Fleet, a frequent visitor to the Taiwan Strait. The United States has been willing to position its warships between China and Taiwan to prevent China from seizing Taiwan by force.

U.S. military support for Taiwan was passed into law by the U.S. Congress in 1979, with the passage of the Taiwan Relations Act (TRA). The TRA states that any threat to Taiwan from China is of grave concern to the United States. That ambiguous phrase hints at the possibility that the United States would intervene on behalf of Taiwan should China ever attack the island.

Support for the defense of Taiwan has been put into practice in a number of ways. During the Korean War, Mao Tse-tung attempted to launch an invasion of Taiwan while the Americans were fighting on the Korean peninsula. The

MR. DEMOCRACY ABROAD

President Lee Tung-hui, Taiwan's first native Taiwanese president, proved to be Taiwan's greatest proponent of the island's transition to democracy. For that, he earned the nickname "Mr. Democracy." Part of President Lee's charm was his willingness to go his own way in the face of criticism. When, for example, he visited his old university in the United States in 1995, he ignored China's threats. The visit was seen by the Chinese government as a dangerous step toward normal diplomatic relations with the United States. And although Lee's visit was a private matter and prompted no change in U.S.-Taiwan relations, China took the opportunity to conduct missile tests in the Taiwan Strait, lobbing shells dangerously close to Taiwan.

Lee's combativeness has continued even after his tenure as president. In June 2000 he traveled to the United Kingdom to attend his daughter's college graduation. China immediately dispatched word to the British that Lee was courting more danger for Taiwan. A spokesman for the Chinese Foreign Ministry, quoted in Taiwan's leading English-language newspaper, the *Taipei Times*, made it clear that China was "strongly opposed to foreign countries giving Lee Tung-hui a platform." Even out of power, Lee rankles the Chinese government. And just as he is known as Mr. Democracy in Taiwan, he is known as "the Old Troublemaker" in Beijing.

United States responded by positioning warships between China and Taiwan. The same maneuver has been repeated a few times since then. When President Lee Tung-hui visited his alma mater, New York State's Cornell University, in 1995, for example, the Chinese began firing missiles near Taiwan. The shelling was ended only by the arrival of the American fleet.

Another result of the TRA is the sale of American military equipment to Taiwan to protect the island against a Chinese invasion. Over the years, the United States has sold Taiwan some of its most advanced fighter craft as well as missiles, radar technology, and other advanced weaponry. The Chinese always condemn these sales, but the United States has refused, so far, to abandon the island.

The result of U.S. military sales to Taiwan is to make a Chinese attack less likely, and so well armed is Taiwan today that it resembles an island fortress. Situated on Taiwan's coastline are warning systems for missile launches and harbors packed with warships. Taiwan also operates sensitive sonar technology to detect submarines nosing around the island. The islands of Matsu and Jinmen are considered the front lines of Taiwan's defensive barrier, and soldiers on both islands outnumber the native inhabitants. To keep a constant state of readiness, Taiwan instituted the draft. All males must serve in the military after high school for two years, and the military offers a good career for anyone who wishes to stay on afterward.

Although Taiwan is tiny compared to China and the Chinese army—the largest standing army in the world, outnumbering the Taiwanese army by six to one—the outcome of a war between China and Taiwan is not a foregone conclusion. One reason for this is because Taiwan's air force is superior to China's and could probably take control of the skies, leaving an invasion force at the mercy of the fighters and bombers overhead. Another problem for the People's Liberation Army is the lack of amphibious assault craft. An American specialist on the Chinese military put it this way: "There's no way at this moment that Beijing has the weapons in its arsenal in sufficient numbers to undertake and sustain a major, full-scale assault on Taiwan."[9]

Eventually, China will probably have the military might to invade Taiwan. In the meantime, it is upgrading its short-range missiles to threaten the Taiwanese. China has fired missiles near Taiwan during the past two presidential elections to scare Taiwanese voters away from voting for a candidate who favors declaring outright independence for Taiwan. The Taiwanese are well aware that China could launch a missile attack at any time, but they have made a choice not to be cowed by their Chinese neighbor.

THE LITTLE TIGER

China's attitude toward Taiwan is not solely one of belliger-ence, however. China has invited many Taiwanese compa-nies to build factories in China, and Taiwan is one of China's greatest sources of investment.

The Taiwanese are extremely proud of their economy, which they have built from almost nothing into a world-class competitor. Taiwan's economy was nearly ruined after World War II. Allied bombs smashed factories and harbors; the Japanese withdrew their experts who ran much of the infra-structure; and the Nationalists dismantled much of what was left. But in the early 1950s, Taiwan began to climb back up the ladder. The economic rebuilding of Taiwan was spurred by U.S. aid, which pumped millions of dollars into Taiwan to prop it up against Communism.

U.S. dollars flooded directly into the coffers of the Nation-alist government, and to their credit, the government spent the money rebuilding Taiwan. The state sponsored industrial development, agricultural modernization, and the budding entrepreneurial class in Taiwan. The Taiwanese love to be their own bosses, and citizens were encouraged to open their own businesses. The result was that small and large business complemented each other, and Taiwan began to outstrip growth in China.

Taiwan took advantage of markets in Asia, especially Japan, to export agricultural goods. Attracted by the promise of cheap labor and lax government regulation, foreign com-panies also set up shop in Taiwan. These new businesses supplied inexpensive manufactured goods to Western mar-kets. Toys in the United States, for example, were rarely seen without a "Made in Taiwan" stamp on the bottom. By the mid-1960s industrial production had tripled from 1953.

In 1964 Taiwan faced a turning point. The United States withdrew economic subsidies, and the Taiwanese were

forced to go it alone. Instead of crippling the economy, the end of U.S. aid spurred a boom in Taiwan's economy. There was a renewed sense of pride in the achievements of the young nation, and with or without U.S. aid, the Taiwanese were determined to be successful. Foreign investment continued to flood Taiwan, and a high demand for Taiwanese products abroad ensured the success of Taiwanese industry.

In the 1970s and 1980s the government continued to modernize Taiwan's infrastructure. Roads were built or modernized, train lines were laid, and harbors were dredged and modernized. Taiwan was running a tight ship, and soon it had become one of the four tiger economies of Asia. Along with Singapore, Hong Kong, and South Korea, Taiwan had caught the attention of world markets.

To hold on to its growing fame for exports, Taiwan began to change over from low-tech, unskilled manufacturing to the high-tech sector. With a tested entrepreneurial class and a large pool of candidates for high-tech jobs, the move was a

Taiwan's pineapple industry has contributed to the enormous success of the country's economy.

The volume of commercial shipping traffic is just one indicator of the attention Taiwan receives from world markets.

success. Taiwan is now the world's leading producer of microchips, which run everything from computers and nuclear reactors to cars and planes.

THE TRAPPINGS OF WEALTH

Today, wealth in Taiwan is remarkably well spread out. Most people fall neatly into the middle class and enjoy the trappings of the modern world: cell phones, televisions, good health care, and modern entertainments. Per capita income has climbed above twelve thousand dollars, and the people of Taiwan have become eager consumers with money to spend. A walk through Taipei or one of the other major cities reveals endless rows of shops selling everything from clothes to electronics. Easy spending money has made the Taiwanese enthusiastic about light entertainments such as karaoke and the cinema.

An average Saturday night in Taiwan for the younger set usually includes a trip to a karaoke establishment. Karaoke, which was imported from Japan, involves singing along to a music video with a microphone while words scrawl across the bottom of a television set. The Taiwanese have gone nuts for karaoke, perhaps because it is something that they can do together, taking turns and having a good laugh at their friends. It retains something of the festive atmosphere of a Taiwanese banquet, and snacks and alcoholic beverages are served.

TAIWANESE CINEMA AND TELEVISION

When not singing karaoke, or perhaps before the karaoke, the Taiwanese love to go to the movies. Theaters have sprouted

Most Taiwanese are middle class and have money to spend in Taiwan's markets and entertainment centers.

up throughout the country and play both domestic films and foreign ones. All films shown in Taiwan have Chinese subtitles and are often dubbed. The reason for the subtitles is the variety of accents and dialects of Chinese-speaking actors and viewers. The film might have been made in Hong Kong, where the dialect, Cantonese, is unintelligible to the Taiwanese. Even if the film is made by Mandarin speakers in Taiwan, there are always those who speak only Taiwanese.

Taiwan's film industry was subsidized by the government, like so many other industries. It has become famous for its productions of historical dramas, stories of revolt against emperors, love stories, and martial arts action movies. Action movies, however, have never been of the frenetic quality of Hong Kong films, and the Taiwanese seem to prefer action mixed with a heavy romantic story line. Dramas with a modern setting are also common, and such films as *Vive l'Amour*, a Taiwanese melodrama, have won international prizes. Taiwan also has its own prize, the Golden Horse, for Mandarin-language films.

Taiwan is also a nation of television watchers. At least one in every three people in Taiwan own a television. The daily fare consists of extremely popular soap operas and multipart historical dramas. Taiwanese television also has a number of political talk shows and news shows to express the varied and heated opinions of Taiwanese politics. As in the United States, television provides a common point of reference in Taiwanese society, and coworkers, friends, and schoolmates frequently talk about the previous day's programming.

TAIWANESE DEMOCRACY

Taiwan's rising standard of living rankles the mainland government in Beijing. The Chinese Communists are irritated that their own system of government has not produced such riches on the mainland. But it has also made China keener to reestablish control over Taiwan.

China's hunger for a richer economy could be seen in 1997, when it reabsorbed the former British colony of Hong Kong, and in 1999, when it reestablished control of the former Portuguese colony of Macao, both of which have much higher economic growth than China. According to China, Taiwan is next.

THE FILMS OF ANG LEE

Taiwan's film industry got a boost when director Ang Lee's films drew worldwide attention. His first three films—*Pushing Hands* (1992), *The Wedding Banquet* (1993), and *Eat Drink Man Woman* (1994)—revealed his keen eye for the subtleties of human relationships. His films focus, like so much in Taiwanese society, on the family relationship and explore subjects like aging, failure in marriage, and homosexuality. Unlike many Taiwanese films, these subjects are not handled in an overly sentimental, melodramatic way, but instead show a sharp sense of humor and poignant interpersonal relationships. *Eat Drink Man Woman* won the Best Picture Award at the Venice Film Vestival in 1994.

In 1995 Lee demonstrated, with *Sense and Sensibility*, that he could also win the admiration of Western audiences. The film is a period piece based on Jane Austen's novel. The film was praised for its remarkable visuals and deft handling of the human comedies involved with the marriage aspirations of young English women of the eighteenth century. Lee's second English-language film, *The Ice Storm* (1997), was another period piece, this time set in an affluent suburban town in the 1970s, and it received lavish praise from American film critics.

Director Ang Lee and actress Kate Winslet on the set of the 1995 movie Sense & Sensibility.

The Taiwanese so far have refused to accept offers to re-unite the economies of China and Taiwan. It is a remarkable feat that Taiwan has thrived economically while constantly under threat of invasion from China and isolated from the rest of the world diplomatically.

The Taiwanese government today is represented through the unofficial Taiwan Economic and Cultural Representative Offices located throughout the world. These offices issue visas, renew passports for Taiwanese citizens, and are staffed by professional diplomats. Although not in name or status, they are Taiwan's consulates and embassies.

It is ironic that Western countries, with their outspoken calls for democracy around the world, refuse to openly support Taiwan, which was the first truly democratic state in Chinese history. But that is the curious position of Taiwan today, neither a nation-state nor a province.

Taiwan's democracy has been propelled by its economic success. As the Taiwanese have prospered, so too have they demanded a greater voice in their own government. Since the legalization of opposition parties in Taiwan, many small parties organized along with the Democratic Progressive Party (DPP), the main opposition party. Among the opposition parties in Taiwan today are the New Party, which is made up of former Nationalist Party members who were fed up with the corruption and inefficiency of the Kuomintang (KMT); the Taiwan Independence Party, which advocates the declaration of independence for Taiwan; the Green Party, a pro-environmental, antinuclear party; and the tiny Labor Party, a left-leaning group that advocates more representation for Taiwan's working class.

In the spring of 2000, Taiwan neared a presidential election. Dissatisfaction with the ruling Nationalist Party was at an all-time high. Not only were citizens fed up with Lee Tung-hui, who was becoming increasingly unpredictable as he aged, but they also accused the KMT of corruption and vote-buying.

The election proved to be Taiwan's most contentious and certainly its most historic to date. President Lee had chosen for his successor Lian Chan, an unpopular KMT official whom Lee had been grooming for the presidency. Lian was resented for his wealth and for the way he was chosen to be the successor. It all smacked of KMT arrogance to many Taiwanese voters.

Opposing Lian was an old KMT member named James Soong. When Soong left the KMT to run as an independent, he took a good slice of the KMT electorate with him. The resulting split in the KMT opened the way for the DPP candidate, Chen Shui-bian, the former mayor of Taipei and a renowned anticorruption advocate.

The election of 2000 presented the first real opportunity for an opposition candidate to win the presidency. Sensing the importance of the election, 83 percent of the Taiwanese electorate turned out to vote. On March 18, Chen Shui-bian was elected president in a close three-way race. Chen's victory marked an end to more than fifty years of Nationalist Party rule and was heralded around the world as a victory for Taiwanese democracy.

THE WIDENING OF THE STRAIT

Along with stunned supporters of the Nationalist Party, who had lived their entire lives under KMT rule, China also expressed anger at Chen's victory. The DPP had long advocated independence for Taiwan and warned Taiwanese voters that war could be the result of a DPP victory.

Chen Shui-bian and his running mate Annette Lu won Taiwan's presidential elections in March 2000, ending more than fifty years of Nationalist rule.

THE LONG STRUGGLE OF CHEN SHUI-BIAN

That Chen Shui-bian could become the president of Taiwan is a signal of how much things have changed since the beginning of Nationalist rule in 1949.

Chen was born in a small village in southern Taiwan and grew up in a mud house with parents who could not read or write. His mother and father worked as day laborers on nearby farms. But Chen excelled in school and eventually won a scholarship to National Taiwan University, the Harvard of Taiwan, and went on to earn a law degree.

Along the road to political power, Chen ran into personal problems and political attacks. As a candidate in 1985 in his native T'ai-nan county, his wife was struck by a speeding motorist and was paralyzed from the waist down. Shortly thereafter, Chen was jailed for libeling a Nationalist government official.

Many voters took these misfortunes to be signs that Chen was willing to sacrifice for his beliefs, and they supported him in his bid to become the mayor of Taipei. As mayor, he gained a reputation for cracking down on corruption, which was rampant in the city. His reputation as a straight arrow also made him a good candidate to oust the ruling Nationalist Party, which people had come to perceive as interested only in retaining power, often through corruption. Chen has earned a place in the history of Taiwanese democracy by becoming the first opposition politician ever elected in the country.

Early in the campaign, however, Chen began backing away from the DPP's independence position. Although he had supported it throughout his career, the stakes were just too high, and he hardly wanted to go down in history as the man who sparked a war with China.

To calm fears in his own country and to placate the Chinese, Chen announced in his first public address that he would not deviate from the current position, the wait-and-see approach to relations with China. He also announced that he was willing to normalize some aspects of the Taiwan-China relationship. He announced that mail could travel directly between China and Taiwan, and he proposed opening direct air and sea links between Matsu and the Chinese province of Fujian. He also suggested the possibility of direct trade and travel links that would eliminate one stop on the usual three-point route to China. Mail, trade, and travel currently pass through a neutral point—usually Hong Kong or South Korea—before moving on to China.

The Chinese responded to all of this with their usual hardball rhetoric. In an official statement, the Chinese government said that anything was possible so long as Chen adhered to the one China policy. And they have made it clear that they are not convinced that he will.

To the Chinese demand, Chen responded, "We can talk about 'one China' as long as it is not a principle. As long as we are treated as equals, there is nothing we cannot discuss."[10] This infuriated the Chinese, who object to dealing with what they consider a province on a state-to-state basis.

Chen further upset the Chinese when he stated, "We won't let Taiwan become another Hong Kong or Macao."[11] Taiwan has moved too far to be simply absorbed by China. Most Taiwanese would rather risk war than be ruled by the Communist government. For now Taiwan is content to live its dangerous existence and focus on the economy and the independent-minded political life of the island. It may be that at some time in the future, Taiwan will have something to teach China about the nature of success in the modern world.

Sun Yat-sen dreamed his entire life of seeing a peaceful Chinese state that allowed Chinese citizens to rule themselves. "I have done my work," he wrote at the end of his life. "The wave of enlightenment and progress cannot now be stayed, and China—the country in the world most fitted to be a republic, because of the industrious and docile character of the people, will in a short time take her place among the civilized and liberty-loving nations of the world."[12] Sun's dream has not yet been realized in China, but in Taiwan, at least, it is a reality.

FACTS ABOUT TAIWAN

GOVERNMENT

Official name: Republic of China, not recognized by most nations; generally called Taiwan

Capital: Taipei

Form of government: Democracy, with a parliamentary bicameral legislature and a directly elected president

Major political parties: Democratic Progressive Party currently in power, Nationalist Party (Kuomintang), New Party

Official language: Mandarin Chinese (referred to as *guoyu* in Taiwan); other common languages include the Taiwanese and Hakka dialects of Chinese

Counties: Taipei, T'aoyuan, Hsin-chu, I-lan, Miao-li, T'ai-chung, Chang-hua, Nan-t'ou, Hua-lien, Yun-lin, Chia-i, T'ai-nan, Kao-hsiung, T'ai-tung, P'ing-tung

Flag: Red with a dark blue rectangle in the upper hoist-side corner bearing a white sun with twelve rectangular rays

PEOPLE

Total population: 22,113,250 (1999 estimate)

Population growth: .93% (1999 estimate)

Most populous city: Taipei, 2,716,000 (1992 estimate)

Other large cities:

Kao-hsiung, 1,398,000 (1992 estimate)

T'ai-chung, 777,000 (1992 estimate)

T'ai-nan, 685,000 (1992 estimate)

Most populous county: Taipei

Population density: 1,503 persons per square mile

Population distribution: urban, 70%; rural, 30%

Ethnic groups: Han Chinese, 98%; aborigines, 2%. The ethnic Chinese people of Taiwan divide themselves into two main groups, both of the same Han Chinese ethnicity. One group calls itself Taiwanese (84% of the general population), who are Chinese people who arrived in Taiwan before the 1949 immigration of the political refugees from the Chinese civil war. The second group is made up of those refugees and their direct descendants (14% of the general population and shrinking due to intermarriage) who arrived in a wave of about 2 million in 1949. The first group (Taiwanese) is referred to in Taiwan as *bensheng ren* (people from the province of Taiwan). The second group is referred to as *waisheng ren* (people from Chinese provinces other than Taiwan).

Aboriginal tribes: Ami, Atayal, Bunun, Paiwan, Puyuma, Rukai, Shao, Saisiat, Tsou, and Yami

Age distribution: 0–14 years, 27.1%; 15–59 years, 63.2%; 60 years and older, 9.7% (1999 estimate)

Life expectancy: males, 74 years; females, 81 years

Births: 15 births per 1,000 persons

Deaths: 5 deaths per 1,000 persons

Infant mortality: 6 deaths per 1,000 live births

Literacy rate: 94%

Compulsory education: 9 years

School attendance rate: 99%

Major religions: Buddhism, Taoism, Confucianism

Suffrage: 20 years of age; universal

HOLIDAYS AND FESTIVALS

Solar calendar public holidays:

January 1	Founding Day
February 28	2/28 day
March 29	Youth Day
April 5	(April 4 during leap years) Tomb Sweeping Day, during which people tend the graves of their ancestors and burn ghost money for the deceased
September 28	Teachers' Day, which is also the birthday of Confucius
October 10	National Day (also known as the Double Ten holiday); celebrates the overthrow of the Ch'ing (Manchu) dynasty in 1911
October 25	Retrocession Day; commemorates the end of Japan's fifty-year occupation of Taiwan
October 31	Chiang Kai-shek's Birthday
November 12	Sun Yat-sen's Birthday
December 25	Constitution Day

Lunar calendar public holidays:

Chinese New Year	Begins on the first day of the first moon
Dragon Boat Festival	Fifth day of the fifth moon
Mid-Autumn Festival	(Also known as the Moon Festival) fifteenth day of the eighth moon

Lunar calendar festivals and cultural events:

Lantern Festival	Fifteenth day of the first moon
Kuanyin's Birthday	Nineteenth day of the second moon; celebration of the goddess of mercy
Matsu's Birthday	Twenty-third day of the third moon; celebration of the goddess of the sea and protector of fishermen

| Ghost Month | Seventh lunar month, an inauspicious time to travel |
| Lovers' Day | Seventh day of the seventh month, similar to St. Valentine's Day |

LAND AND CLIMATE

Location: Eastern Asia, islands bordering the East China Sea, Philippine Sea, South China Sea, and Taiwan Strait; north of the Philippines; off the southeastern coast of China

Area:
    Total: 13,892 square miles (35,980 square kilometers)
    Land: 12,456 square miles (32,260 square kilometers)
    Water: 1,263 square miles (3,720 square kilometers)

Nearest neighbor: China

Major islands: Jinmen, Matsu, Wu-ch'iu, P'eng-hu (Pescadores), Liu-ch'iu, Green, Orchid

Coastline: 900 miles (1,448 kilometers)

Climate: tropical, marine; rainy season during southwest monsoon (June to August); cloudiness is persistent and extensive all year

Terrain: Eastern two-thirds is mostly rugged mountains; flat to gently rolling plains in west

Elevation extremes:
    Lowest point: South China Sea, 0 feet (0 meters)
    Highest point: Yü Shan, 13,114 feet (3,997 meters)

Natural resources: Small deposits of coal, natural gas, limestone, marble, and asbestos

Land use:
    Arable land: 24%
    Permanent crops: 1%
    Permanent pastures: 5%
    Forests and woodland: 55%
    Other: 15%

Natural hazards: Earthquakes and typhoons

Environmental Issues: Air pollution; water pollution from industrial emissions, raw sewage; contamination of drinking water supplies; trade in endangered species; low-level radioactive waste disposal

ECONOMY

Official currency: New Taiwan dollar

Exchange rate: US $1 = NT $30.83 (June 2000)

Gross domestic product (GDP): $362 billion (1998 estimate)

GDP real growth rate: 4.8% (1998 estimate)

GDP by sector:
    Agriculture 2.7%
    Industry 35.3%
    Services 62%

Major industries: textiles, clothing, electronics, processed foods, chemicals, plastics

Chief crops: rice, bananas, pineapples, sugarcane, sweet potatoes, peanuts

Labor force: 15% agricultural, 53% industry and commerce, 22% services

Unemployment rate 2.7% (1998)

Exports: 122.1 billion (1997)

Imports: 114.4 billion (1997)

Major trading partners:

    Imports: Japan, 30%; United States, 23%

    Exports: United States, 39%; Japan 13%; China 8%

Telephones: 1 telephone per 3 persons

Televisions: 1 television per 3.2 persons

Radios: 1 radio per 1.5 persons

Daily newspaper circulation: 202 newspapers per 1,000 population (1989 estimate)

WEIGHTS AND MEASURES

Length:
    The Chinese "foot" is called a *chir*
    1 *chir* = 11.9 inches, or 0.99 feet = 0.30 meters
    1 *jang* = 10 *chir*

Weight:
    The Chinese "pound" is called a *catty* or *jin*
    1 *jin* = 1.32 pounds, or 0.6 kilograms = 21.2 ounces or 37.5 grams
    The Chinese "ounce" is called a *liang*
    1 *liang* = 1.32 ounces or 37.5 grams

Area:
    The Chinese units of measure for area are the *ping* and *jia*
    1 *ping* = 36 square feet
    1 *jia* = 2.40 acres

NOTES

CHAPTER 3: A PRIZE FOR KINGS AND EMPERORS

1. Daniel Reid et al., *Insight Guide: Taiwan*. Singapore: APA Publications, 1998, p. 26.

2. Jonathan D. Spence, *The Search for Modern China*. New York: W. W. Norton, 1990, p. 54.

3. Quoted in Reid, *Insight Guide: Taiwan*, p. 32.

4. Spence, *The Search for Modern China*, p. 454.

CHAPTER 4: A REPUBLIC IN EXILE

5. Fred W. Riggs, *Formosa Under Chinese Nationalist Rule*. New York: Macmillan, 1952, p. 42.

6. John F. Copper, *Taiwan: Nation-State or Province?* 3rd ed. Boulder, CO: Westview, 1999, p. 43.

7. Copper, *Taiwan*, p. 47.

CHAPTER 5: TAIWAN TODAY

8. Quoted in Reid, *Insight Guide*, p. 82.

CHAPTER 6: AN UNFINISHED STORY

9. Quoted in Craig Smith, "Behind China's Threats," *New York Times*, March 7, 2000, p. A1.

10. Quoted in Erik Eckholm, "What Now for Beijing and Taipei?" *New York Times*, March 21, 2000, p. A8.

11. Quoted in Erik Eckholm, "Taiwan Nationalists Ousted After Half-Century Reign," *New York Times*, March 19, 2000, p. A1.

12. Quoted in Stephen Chen and Robert Payne, *Sun Yat-sen: A Portrait*. New York: John Day, 1946, pp. 224–25.

CHRONOLOGY

PRE-1400s
Taiwan is inhabited by tribes of Malayo-Polynesian aborigines.

CA. 1400
Emigrants from China's Fujian province begin to settle in Taiwan.

1544
The Portuguese land in Taiwan and dub it Ilha Formosa, "the Beautiful Island."

1624
The Dutch erect Fort Zeelandia on an islet, named Taiwan, close to today's T'ai-nan City, and begin to colonize the southwestern part of the island.

1626
The Spanish settle in northern Taiwan and build Fort Santo Domingo.

1642
The Dutch expel the Spanish from northern Taiwan.

1653
The Dutch build Fort Provintia in today's T'ai-nan City after Chinese immigrants' unsuccessful rebellion.

1661
After being defeated by the Manchus in China, Koxinga, the last general of the Ming Dynasty, leads twenty-five thousand nobles, soldiers, and pirates to invade Taiwan.

1662
After a siege of nine months and the loss of sixteen hundred Dutch lives, the Dutch governor surrenders Taiwan to Koxinga; Koxinga dies four months later and his son succeeds him as king of Taiwan.

1683
Manchus lead by Shi Lang, one of Koxinga's former officers,   95

annihilate the kingdom of Taiwan and annex western Taiwan to the Chinese empire.

1867
John Dodd, a pioneer of Taiwan's tea industry, rents two clipper ships and begins exporting Formosa oolong tea to New York.

1884
French forces invade northern Taiwan and occupy Chi-lung.

1885
Coubert occupies the P'eng-hu Islands with a vision to transform them into France's Hong Kong; he dies of a tropical disease in June; French forces withdraw from the Chi-lung area and the P'eng-hu Islands.

1887
The Chinese annex Taiwan, giving it provincial status.

1895
China cedes Taiwan to Japan in the Treaty of Shimonoseki, which ends the Sino-Japanese War; the Taiwanese establish the first republic in Asia to resist impending Japanese rule.

1898
Kodama Gentaro becomes the fourth governor-general of Taiwan; he appoints Goto Shimpei as chief administrator; Taiwan begins its painful modernization.

1902
The legendary anti-Japanese leader Lim Siau-niau and his followers are killed while defending their stronghold, Au Pia Na, near Kao-hsiung; this marks the end of open military resistance of Taiwanese people against Japanese rule.

1911
The Ch'ing Dynasty is overthrown; the Republic of China is established.

1927–1949
Chinese civil war between Chinese Nationalists and Communists.

1937
Japan invades China, and World War II begins in Asia; Taiwan is an important staging area for Japanese troops.

1943

Cairo Declaration is issued by the United States and Britain, promising to "restore" Taiwan to China.

1945

World War II ends; Taiwan returns to Nationalist rule; Republic of China signs UN Charter and becomes founding member of the UN.

1947

Chinese rule brings widespread corruption to the government, chaos to society, and runaway inflation to the economy; on February 28, a general uprising breaks out; Chiang Kai-shek sends in troops from China and conducts ruthless suppression; twenty thousand Taiwanese are massacred by Nationalist troops.

1949

China's civil war ends; Nationalists flee to Taiwan; People's Republic of China (PRC) is established; PRC lays claim to Taiwan.

1949–1987

Chiang Kai-shek establishes martial law in Taiwan.

1950

Korean War begins; United States sends Seventh Fleet to the Taiwan Strait.

1951

San Francisco Peace Treaty establishes legal basis for Taiwanese self-determination.

1971

Taiwan's seat in the UN is given to the People's Republic of China.

1972

The Shanghai Communiqué establishes normal relations between the United States and China.

1975

Chiang Kai-shek dies.

1978

Chiang Ching-kuo, Chiang Kai-shek's son, becomes president of the Republic of China (ROC).

1979

The United States recognizes the PRC, ending the recognition of the ROC; United States signs the Taiwan Relations Act to protect the welfare of Taiwan; the violent suppression of an opposition rally by the Nationalists, known as the Kao-hsiung Incident, occurs.

1980s

Chiang Ching-kuo's government focuses on development, fostering Taiwan's economic boom.

1986

The Democratic Progressive Party (DPP)—Taiwan's first opposition party—is formed.

1987

Martial law is lifted.

1988

Chiang Ching-kuo dies; the Nationalist Party appoints Lee Tung-hui president of Taiwan, making him the first Taiwan-born leader of the island under the Nationalists; Taiwanese are allowed to visit mainland China for the first time in forty years.

1991

Independence platform is adopted by the DPP; the Nationalist Party abandons its claim to be the only legitimate government of China, saying instead that it leads one of two equal governments; Beijing denounces this as separatism.

1992

The DPP gains one-third of the seats in parliamentary elections.

1993

The UN rejects Taiwan's membership application.

1995

Taiwanese president Lee Tung-hui makes a private visit to Cornell University; Beijing is alarmed that a Taiwanese leader has been given a U.S. visa and holds missile exercises in the Taiwan Strait.

1996

Lee Tung-hui is elected president by popular vote; China deploys 150,000 troops on the mainland near Taiwan and begins missile tests aimed at influencing the Taiwanese elections; the United States sends two carrier groups to the region to prevent further escalation.

1998
U.S. President Bill Clinton visits China and says the United States does not support Taiwan's independence; some Taiwanese see Clinton's statement as damaging their right to self-determination; the Clinton administration claims there has been no change in U.S. policy toward Taiwan.

2000
Chen Shui-bian is elected president, becoming the first Taiwanese leader elected from an opposition party, thereby ending fifty years of rule by the Nationalist Party; in his first speech, he abandons his party's pro-independence platform and eases tensions with the Communist mainland.

Suggestions for Further Reading

Baedeker's China. New York: Macmillan Travel, 1996. A detailed travel guide to the People's Republic of China (with a chapter on Taiwan), including essays on China's topography, economy, history, and arts and culture.

Cao Xueqin, *The Story of the Stone (The Dream of the Red Chamber).* 5 vols. New York: Penguin, 1973–1986. China's most famous classical novel.

Confucius, *The Analects of Confucius.* Trans. Arthur Waley. New York: Vintage, 1983. The writings of China's greatest philosopher.

Arthur Cotterell, *China: A Cultural History.* New York: Mentor, 1990. An engaging overview of Chinese civilization from the earliest days to the founding of the People's Republic of China.

Robert Green, *Modern Nations of the World: China.* San Diego: Lucent Books, 1999. A book from the same series on the Chinese motherland.

Stephen G. Haw, *A Traveller's History of China.* New York: Interlink Books, 1997. A well-written, concise overview of Chinese history and modern Chinese society.

Yuan Ke, *Dragons and Dynasties: An Introduction to Chinese Mythology.* Trans. Kim Echlin and Nie Zhixiong. New York: Penguin, 1993. An explanation of old Chinese cosmology and a retelling of myths and folktales from China.

Henry Pu Yi, *The Last Manchu: The Autobiography of Henry Pu Yi, Last Emperor of China.* Ed. Paul Kramer. Trans. Kuo Ying Paul Tsai. New York: Pocket Books, 1987. The autobiography of China's last emperor written at the request of the Chinese Communists, who had captured Pu Yi and forced him to write about his life in prison. The book is a remarkable first-hand account of the life inside the Forbidden City as well as a chronicle of the political upheaval of twentieth-century China.

Eduardo del Rius, *Mao for Beginners.* New York: Pantheon Books, 1980. An entertaining and informative summary of Mao Tse-tung's life and his beliefs by the left-leaning Mexican journalist Rius.

Sterling Seagrave, *The Soong Dynasty.* New York: Harper & Row, 1986. A revealing portrait of one of China's most influential families, with much biographical information on the rise of the Nationalist Party and Chiang Kai-shek, the founder of Taiwan.

Jonathan D. Spence and Annping Chin, *The Chinese Century: A Photographic History of the Last Hundred Years.* New York: Random House, 1996. An oversize volume of photographs and essays from about 1900 to the Tiananmen square incident.

Sun Zi (Sun Tzu), *The Art of War.* New York: Delacorte, 1983. The celebrated work of Chinese military strategy, written by a fifth-century B.C. general.

WORKS CONSULTED

Books

Chris and Ling-li Bates, *Culture Shock: Taiwan: A Guide to Customs and Etiquette.* Portland, OR: Graphic Arts Center, 1995. An introduction to the social landscape of Taiwan, this book provides foreigners with a guide to avoiding the unpleasant side of culture clash in Taiwan.

Stephen Chen and Robert Payne, *Sun Yat-sen: A Portrait.* New York: John Day, 1946. A biography of the tireless proponent of a Chinese republic. Sun is still regarded as a founding father by both the Communist mainland and Nationalist Taiwan.

John F. Copper, *Historical Dictionary of Taiwan.* Metuchen, NJ: Scarecrow, 1993. Contains alphabetical entries on modern Taiwanese figures and events, with a historical introduction and time line.

———, *Taiwan: Nation-State or Province?* 3rd ed. Boulder, CO: Westview, 1999. This concise book explores the dispute between mainland China and Taiwan over the role of Taiwan.

John King Fairbank, *The United States and China.* Cambridge, MA: Harvard University Press, 1979. A scholarly introduction to modern China and Chinese-American relations.

Sven Hedin, *Chiang Kai-shek: Marshal of China.* Trans. Bernard Norbelie. New York: Da Capo, 1975. An unabashedly adulatory biography of Chiang Kai-shek, which provides an interesting insight into his unexamined reputation before his death.

George H. Kerr, *Formosa: Licensed Revolution and the Home Rule Movement, 1895–1945.* Honolulu: University of Hawaii Press, 1974. A study of the effects of Japanese occupation on Taiwan's industry and society.

Douglas Mendel, *The Politics of Formosan Nationalism.* Berkeley and Los Angeles: University of California Press,

1970. An examination of the rise of pro-independence nationalism in Taiwan and antimainland sentiment directed at both the Communists and the Nationalists.

Raymon H. Myers, ed., *Two Societies in Opposition: The Republic of China and the People's Republic of China After Forty Years.* Stanford, CA: Hoover Institution, 1991. A collection of essays looking at the changes in Taiwan-China relations and how the two societies have changed during their fifty years of separation.

Daniel Reid et al., *Insight Guide: Taiwan.* Singapore: APA Publications, 1998. A self-described "visual travel book," this Insight Guide provides essays on Taiwanese history and culture with descriptions of some central tourist sights on the island and many attractive photographs.

Fred W. Riggs, *Formosa Under Chinese Nationalist Rule.* New York: Macmillan, 1952. A detailed study of the first decade of Nationalist rule in China, which undercuts some of the myths created by international praise for the Nationalist government in its earliest years.

James E. Sheridan, *China in Disintegration: The Republican Era in Chinese History, 1912–1949.* New York: Free, 1975. A history of the 1911 revolution and the Chinese civil war between the Nationalists and the Communists.

Douglas C. Smith, *The Yami of Lan-Yu Island: Portrait of a Culture in Transition.* Bloomington, IN: Phi Delta Kappa Educational Foundation, 1998. A study of the ancient inhabitants of Lan Yü Island, located off the east coast of Taiwan.

Jonathan D. Spence, *The Search for Modern China.* New York: W. W. Norton, 1990. An in-depth study of the forces that shaped modern China, from the Ming dynasty to the protests at Tiananmen Square. Spence is undoubtedly the most famous living China scholar writing in English.

Robert Storey, *Taiwan.* Hawthorn, Australia: Lonely Planet, 1998. A comprehensive guidebook to Taiwan, including information on language, culture, history, and the surrounding islands.

Barbara W. Tuchman, *Stilwell and the American Experience in China, 1911–45.* New York: Bantam Books, 1972. A fascinating portrait of "Vinegar" Joe Stilwell, the highest-ranking

U.S. general in China during World War II, and a history of American relations with the Nationalist Chinese government.

Willem Van Kemenade, *China, Hong Kong, Taiwan, Inc.* New York: Knopf, 1997. A study of the interplay among three distinct Chinese economies.

Periodicals

Erik Eckholm, "Taiwan Nationalists Ousted After Half-Century Reign," *New York Times*, March 19, 2000.

————, "What Now for Beijing and Taipei?" *New York Times*, March 21, 2000.

Craig Smith, "Behind China's Threats," *New York Times*, March 7, 2000.

INDEX